Contents

Licence

Text © Pat Hoodless

© 2003 Scholastic Ltd

Published by Scholastic Ltd, Villiers House,
Clarendon Avenue, Leamington Spa,
Warwickshire CV32 5PR

Printed by Bell & Bain Ltd, Glasgow

567890   89012

British Library Cataloguing-in-Publication Data
A catalogue record for this book is available from
the British Library.

ISBN 0-439-98454-8

Visit our website at
www.scholastic.co.uk

CD Developed in association with
Footmark Media Ltd

Author
Pat Hoodless

Editor
Clare Gallaher

Assistant Editor
Roanne Charles

Series Designer
Joy Monkhouse

Designer
Catherine Mason

Cover photographs
© Photodisc,
© Stockbyte

 # Acknowledgements

Every effort has been made to trace copyright holders and the publishers apologise for any omissions.

 Made with Macromedia is a
trademark of Macromedia, Inc.
Director ®
Copyright © 1984-2000
Macromedia, Inc.

Minimum Specifications:
PC: Windows 98 SE or higher
Processor: Pentium 2 (or equivalent) 400 MHz
RAM: 128 Mb
CD-ROM drive: 48x (52x preferred)

MAC: OS 9.2 (OSX preferred)
Processor: G3 400 MHz
RAM: 128Mb
CD-ROM drive: 48x (52x preferred)

List of resources on the CD-ROM

The page numbers refer to the teacher's notes provided in this book.

Ancient Greeks

Indus Valley

Tudor exploration

INTRODUCTION

This book and CD-ROM support the teaching and learning set out in the QCA Scheme of Work for history in Years 5 and 6. The CD provides a large bank of varied visual resources. The book provides teacher's notes, background information, ideas for discussion and activities to accompany the CD resources, along with photocopiable pages to support teaching and learning. All have been specially chosen to meet the requirements outlined in the QCA units on Ancient Greece and Greek ideas, the Indus Valley civilisation and the effects of Tudor exploration. Additional resources and ideas have also been included to enable teachers to broaden these areas of study if they wish, such as stories and personal accounts. The resources are also relevant and useful to those not necessarily following the QCA Schemes of Work, particularly teachers in Scotland.

The resources and activities are not intended to be used rigidly, however, since they do not provide a structure for teaching in themselves. The teacher's notes provide ideas for discussion and activities that focus on the 'Knowledge, skills and understanding' of the National Curriculum for history. They aim to guide teachers in developing the skills and concepts that are fundamental to children's understanding of what it is to learn about the past.

In this book, there is an emphasis on developing children's awareness and understanding of chronology, of asking and answering questions, and of investigating historical sources and communicating findings in a variety of ways. Above all, the activities and discussions aim to build clear links between the first-hand experience they gain from using the resources on the CD and their developing awareness of the past.

Links with other subjects
Literacy
There are a number of close links between the topics covered in this book and work on literacy. The discussion activities contribute directly to the requirements for speaking and listening, as do the drama and role-play activities. The stories may be used in shared reading during the Literacy Hour or to provide a stimulus for shared, guided or independent writing. There is considerable opportunity for the children to develop their creative writing skills in the form of historical stories or information texts. Images from the CD could be printed to stimulate independent writing or to illustrate it. They may also be used to illustrate the timelines or sequence lines created in the course of each topic.

Geography
In discussing issues and events concerning Ancient Greece, the Indus Valley and Tudor exploration, geographical links are indispensable. Consequently, there is considerable emphasis on the use and interpretation of maps, as part of the contextual background for topics.

Art and design
There are similarly close links with art. For example, in making imaginative pictures of historical figures and places, such as Ancient Greek scholars and Olympia, children are representing and developing their understanding of historical contexts. They also look at sculpture, particularly in the form of statues of historical figures, and architecture, for example the Acropolis. Through examining the images provided on the CD, children will naturally become involved in discussion of the ideas, methods and techniques used by artists. They will also begin to appreciate the roles and functions of art at different times, particularly its importance as a historical source.

Design and technology
Examination of the resources on the CD and discussion about them generates investigation of various design and technology topics in a historical context.

ICT
Finally, there are clear links with information technology. ICT is constantly useful throughout these activities, particularly in terms of providing an inexhaustible resource for children to use in carrying out research into specific aspects of each topic. There are also opportunities for children to communicate their findings through the use of ICT.

HOW TO USE THE CD-ROM

Windows NT users

If you use Windows NT you may see the following error message: 'The procedure entry point Process32First could not be located in the dynamic link library KERNEL32.dll'. Click on **OK** and the CD will autorun with no further problems.

Setting up your computer for optimal use

On opening, the CD will alert you if changes are needed in order to operate the CD at its optimal use. There are three changes you may be advised to make:

Viewing resources at their maximum screen size

To see images at their maximum screen size, your screen display needs to be set to 800 x 600 pixels. In order to adjust your screen size you will need to **Quit** the program.

If using a PC, open the **Control Panel**. Select **Display** and then **Settings**. Adjust the **Desktop Area** to 800 x 600 pixels. Click on **OK** and then restart the program.

If using a Mac, from the **Apple** menu select **Control Panels** and then **Monitors** to adjust the screen size.

Adobe Acrobat Reader

To print high-quality versions of images and to view and print the photocopiable pages on the CD you need **Adobe Acrobat Reader** installed on your computer. If you do not have it installed already, a version is provided on the CD. To install this version **Quit** the 'Ready Resources' program.

If using a PC, right-click on the **Start** menu on your desktop and choose **Explore**. Click on the **+** sign to the left of the CD drive entitled 'Ready Resources' and open the folder called 'Acrobat Reader Installer'. Run the program contained in this folder to install **Adobe Acrobat Reader**.

If using a Mac, double click on the 'Ready Resources' icon on the desktop and on the 'Acrobat Reader Installer' folder. Run the program contained in this folder to install **Adobe Acrobat Reader**.

PLEASE NOTE: If you do not have **Adobe Acrobat Reader** installed, you will not be able to print high-quality versions of images, or to view or print photocopiable pages (although these are provided in the accompanying book and can be photocopied).

QuickTime

In order to view the videos and listen to the audio on this CD you will need to have **QuickTime version 5 or later** installed on your computer. If you do not have it installed already or have an older version of QuickTime, the latest version can be downloaded at http://www.apple.com/quicktime/download/win.html. If you choose to install this version, **Quit** the 'Ready Resources' program.

PLEASE NOTE: If you do not have **QuickTime** installed you will be unable to view the films.

Menu screen

▶ Click on the **Resource Gallery** of your choice to view the resources available under that topic.

▶ Click on **Complete Resource Gallery** to view all the resources available on the CD.

▶ Click on **Photocopiable Resources (PDF format)** to view a list of the photocopiables provided in the book that accompanies this CD.

▶ **Back**: click to return to the **opening screen**. Click **Continue** to move to the **Menu screen**.

▶ **Quit**: click **Quit** to close the menu program and progress to the **Quit screen.** If you quit from the **Quit screen** you will exit the CD. If you do not quit you will return to the **Menu screen**.

Resource Galleries

▶ **Help**: click **Help** to find support on accessing and using images.

▶ **Back to menu:** click here to return to the **Menu screen**.

▶ **Quit:** click here to move to the **Quit screen** – see **Quit** above.

Viewing images

Small versions of each image are shown in the Resource Gallery. Click and drag the slider on the slide bar to scroll through the images in the Resource Gallery, or click on the arrows to

move the images frame by frame. Roll the pointer over an image to see the caption.
▶ Click on an image to view the screen-sized version of it.
▶ To return to the Resource Gallery click on **Back to Resource Gallery**.

Viewing videos

Click on the video icon of your choice in the Resource Gallery. In order to view the videos on this CD, you will need to have **QuickTime** installed on your computer (see 'Setting up your computer for optimal use' above).

Once at the video screen, use the buttons on the bottom of the video screen to operate the video. The slide bar can be used for a fast forward and rewind. To return to the Resource Gallery click on **Back to Resource Gallery**.

Listening to sound recordings

Click on the required sound icon. Use the buttons or the slide bar to hear the sound. A transcript will be displayed on the viewing screen where appropriate. To return to the Resource Gallery, click on **Back to Resource Gallery**.

Printing

Click on the image to view it (see 'Viewing images' above). There are two print options:

Print using Acrobat enables you to print a high-quality version of an image. Choosing this option means that the image will open as a read-only page in **Adobe Acrobat** and in order to access these files you will need to have already installed **Adobe Acrobat Reader** on your computer (see 'Setting up your computer for optimal use' above). To print the selected resource, select **File** and then **Print**. Once you have printed the resource **minimise** or **close** the Adobe screen using — or **X** in the top right-hand corner of the screen. Return to the Resource Gallery by clicking on **Back to Resource Gallery**.

Simple print enables you to print a lower quality version of the image without the need to use **Adobe Acrobat Reader**. Select the image and click on the **Simple print** option. After printing, click on **Back to Resource Gallery**.

Slideshow presentation

If you would like to present a number of resources without having to return to the Resource Gallery and select a new image each time, you can compile a slideshow. Click on the **+** tabs at the top of each image in the Resource Gallery you would like to include in your presentation (pictures, sound and video can be included). It is important that you click on the images in the order in which you would like to view them (a number will appear on each tab to confirm the order). If you would like to change the order, click on **Clear slideshow** and begin again. Once you have selected your images – up to a maximum of 20 – click on **Play slideshow** and you will be presented with the first of your selected resources. To move to the next selection in your slideshow click on **Next slide**, to see a previous resource click on **Previous slide**. You can end your slideshow presentation at any time by clicking on **Resource Gallery**. Your slideshow selection will remain selected until you **Clear slideshow** or return to the **Menu screen**.

Viewing on an interactive whiteboard or data projector

Resources can be viewed directly from the CD. To make viewing easier for a whole class, use a large monitor, data projector or interactive whiteboard. For group, paired or individual work, the resources can be viewed from the computer screen.

Photocopiable resources (PDF format)

To view or print a photocopiable resource page, click on the required title in the list and the page will open as a read-only page in **Adobe Acrobat**. In order to access these files you will need to have already installed **Adobe Acrobat Reader** on your computer (see 'Setting up your computer for optimal use' above). To print the selected resource select **File** and then **Print**. Once you have printed the resource **minimise** or **close** the Adobe screen using — or **X** in the top right-hand corner of the screen. This will take you back to the list of PDF files. To return to the **Menu screen**, click on **Back**.

Technical support

For all technical support queries, please phone Scholastic Customer Services on **0845 603 9091**.

ANCIENT GREEKS

Content, skills and concepts

This chapter relates to units 14 and 15 of the QCA Scheme of Work for history at Key Stage 2, and will assist teachers in planning and researching work on the topics of the Ancient Greeks and the influence of Ancient Greek ideas today. Together with the Ancient Greeks Resource Gallery on the CD, it introduces a range of sources, including photographs of statues, maps, illustrations of scenes from everyday life, accounts, stories and a playscript. The chapter also provides materials to support the teaching of key historical concepts relevant to this period and theme.

Children will already have gained experience, while working on other history units, of sequencing and using timelines, the use of time-related vocabulary, asking and answering questions, and using visual, written and auditory sources. Recounting stories about the past, and looking for similarities and differences between the past and the present, are prior learning activities which will have introduced relevant skills and concepts to the children before they progress to the skills and concepts in this unit. The chapter includes suggestions for the extension of other skills, such as recognising change and continuity, and the ability to select and use information to support an argument.

Resources on the CD-ROM

A map, photographs of modern day Greece, ancient remains and artefacts, illustrations, and pictures of statues are provided on the CD. Direct comparisons will be possible between the ancient past and the present day to better enable the children to understand the legacy of Ancient Greek traditions and ideas. Teacher's notes containing background information about these sources are provided in this chapter, along with ideas for further work on them.

Photocopiable pages

Photocopiable resources are provided within the book and in PDF format on the CD from which they can be printed. They include:
▶ word and sentence cards
▶ a timeline
▶ stories, biographies, descriptions
▶ a playscript.

The teacher's notes that accompany the photocopiable pages include suggestions for developing discussion about the pages and for ways of using them for whole class, group or individual activities.

History skills

Skills such as observing, describing, using time-related vocabulary, sequencing, using a timeline, understanding the meaning of dates including BC and AD, comparing, inferring, listening, speaking, reading, writing and drawing are all involved in the activities suggested, for both the resources on the CD and the photocopiable pages. For example, there is an opportunity to develop independent sequencing skills through the use of the timeline of the main events during the Ancient Greek period. The children can learn to use descriptive vocabulary to describe the maps, pictures, illustrations and statues shown on the CD.

Historical understanding

In the course of the suggested tasks, a further aim is for children to develop a more detailed knowledge of the past and sequence and date events independently, through their understanding of the context and content of the factual information they use. They will begin to give reasons for events, use sources to find further information and be able to recount and rewrite stories and accounts they have heard, sometimes using different forms of presentation. They will also have the opportunity to extend their skills in using descriptive language and specific time-related terms to write their own factual accounts of the past. Communication skills of various types can also be practised and developed.

NOTES ON THE CD-ROM RESOURCES

Ancient Greek Empire

Greece in the 5th and early 4th centuries BC was dominated by the city state of Athens. There was also another city state, Sparta, in the Peloponnese. The two city states of Athens and Sparta were fierce rivals, with their own cultures, beliefs, laws, rulers and money. Between 431 and 404BC the two states waged the Peloponnesian War. This culminated in the defeat of Athens and an end to her dominance in Ancient Greece.

The final blow for Athens, however, came from the state of Macedonia when their leader Philip II began a campaign of conquest and subordinated all of Greece. His son was Alexander the Great and he carried on with his father's campaign of conquest to become Greece's most famous ruler. This map shows the extent of the Greek Empire at the time of Alexander the Great. Between 334 and 323BC, Alexander extended Greek rule into north Africa and into the Middle and Far East, defeating the Persian Empire. The new Greek Empire took in parts of modern day Iraq and Iran and reached into the Far East to modern day Bangladesh. It is interesting to note how Alexander liked to highlight the expansion of his empire by naming many of the principal cities he conquered after himself. This explains the many different towns called Alexandria, or another version of his name, that can be seen on this map.

Discussing the map

▶ Look carefully at the map of Ancient Greece at the time of Alexander the Great. Ask the class what they notice about it, for example its size and the areas of the world it covered.
▶ Note the number of places that were all called Alexandria, and ask the children why they think this was.
▶ Ask the children what they think Alexander had done, for example conquered these areas.
▶ Explain that Alexander fought against and defeated the Persian Empire, and this meant that he then controlled all their lands.
▶ Discuss the position of Sparta in relation to Athens; explain that Sparta was inland and Athens near the coast. How might this affect how each lived? Discuss how the two cultures developed in different ways and how the two city states were always enemies.

Activities

▶ Help the children to locate the period of Alexander's war against Persia on the timeline of Ancient Greece (see photocopiable page 30).
▶ Get the children to compare a modern day map with this one, and to identify some of the places that were taken over by Alexander the Great.
▶ Challenge them to search for further information about Alexander, and set each child the task of writing a short biography of him. Look at the examples of biographies of the Ancient Greek scholars on photocopiable pages 36–8, and discuss the meaning of the word *biography*.
▶ Set small groups the task of searching for information about the Persian Empire, Asia, Egypt and the Indus Valley at the time of Alexander. Suggest that they find four or five facts about each place to pass on to other groups at a given time. They could use library resources or the Internet for their research.
▶ Tell the class the history of Athens and Sparta and introduce them to the Peloponnesian War. Challenge each child to research and then write a short paragraph about both Athens and Sparta.

Modern day Athens

This photograph shows the city of Athens as it is in modern times. It is taken looking towards Likavitos Hill from the Hill of the Acropolis, just two of the many hills in and around Athens. This view does not show any of the significant historic features of Athens, but it does illustrate the density of the modern population. Tall, closely packed buildings fill every available piece of low-lying land, leaving the steep-sided hills exposed. In contrast, the important ancient buildings, like many Greek churches today, were located on top of hills or their slopes – in particular the Hill of the Acropolis itself, where there is the Parthenon, the Erechtheum, the Temple of Athena Nike, Odeons of Pericles and Herodes Atticus, and the Theatre of Dionysos, among other ancient buildings.

Discussing the photograph
▶ Ask the children if they have ever been to Athens and what they already know about it.
▶ Ask if they know what is special about Athens, for example that it is the capital city of Greece; its history.
▶ Ask if they know of any famous places in Athens, and tell them about the Parthenon and the Acropolis.
▶ Look closely at the photograph of modern day Athens, and ask what they notice first about it, for example they may point out the modern buildings. Explain that this is a view of one of the hills in Athens, taken from the Acropolis Hill. Ask if anyone can see any ancient buildings or sites on this photograph.
▶ Discuss how busy modern Athens is and about the air pollution that is becoming a serious problem there. Ask if they can explain why Athens may be experiencing these problems.

Activities
▶ Explain how Athens was, for a time, the leading city state, or 'polis', in Ancient Greece, and how this period lasted between about 593 and 404BC. Help the children to locate this on the timeline of Ancient Greece (see photocopiable page 30) and the map showing the 'Ancient Greek Empire' (provided on the CD).
▶ During a shared writing session, discuss and write some of the key reasons why Athens was so important during this time – its position near the coast; its seafaring and trade; its democratic tradition, and so on.
▶ Ask the children to bring to school a selection of travel brochures for Greece and Athens, and to make notes about the main features of Athens using these. Set the class the task of producing their own short travel brochure about Athens. Alternatively, they could design posters advertising the attractions of Athens and make a travel display.

Dodecane

There are many small Greek islands scattered in the Mediterranean and Aegean Seas. Some islands are grouped together, such as those known as the Dodecanese islands. This group is to be found just off the coast of Turkey and north of the island of Crete. The islands of the Dodecanese include Rhodes, Kos, Simi, Tilos, Kalymnos, Nissiros, Astipalaia, Kassos, Leros, Kastelorizo, Halki, Patmos, Lipsi and Karpathos. Known today as tourist resorts, these islands have warm, sunny climates during the summer months and are considered among some of the most beautiful in Greece.

Discussing the photograph
▶ Ask how many children have been to a Greek island on holiday, and discuss what is distinctive about them. Talk about why people like to go on holiday there.
▶ Look at the photograph, and explain that it is a view of an island in the Dodecanese group of islands.
▶ List some of the Dodecanese islands for the class.
▶ Tell the children a little about the history of the Dodecanese islands, for example they were often controlled by different powers, such as the Persian Empire, the Roman Empire, the Byzantine Empire, and the Venetians as well as Ancient Greece, and how this has given the islands a very multicultural past and present.
▶ Ask the class to list the features of the Dodecanese that they think are important.

Activities
▶ Use a large-scale map of Greece and ask for volunteers to locate the Dodecanese islands, identifying individual islands that they may have visited.
▶ Collect books and travel guides about Greece and set the children, working in pairs, the task of finding information about selected islands. Ask them to make notes and use their notes to give talks or to write short descriptive pieces about their chosen island.
▶ Provide painting materials for the children to make their own posters advertising their chosen island.

Battle scene on vase

This ancient Greek vase shows the importance of warfare in the lives of the Ancient Greeks. Leaders who decided on a war would be expected to fight alongside the men. Fighting at a distance was considered weak by the Ancient Greeks, who prided themselves on their skills in hand-to-hand combat. Greek warriors, or hoplites, are shown on the left of this picture, wearing metal, crested helmets. They carried a shield, spear and short sword in battle and although they are shown here unencumbered by heavy clothing, they would often wear body armour made of bronze or of linen reinforced with metal. The amount and quality of armour that a soldier wore depended on his resources, since it had to be provided by the soldier himself. Fathers would sometimes provide armour for their sons when they entered the army.

Discussing the photograph
▶ Ask the children what type of object is shown in this photograph. Talk about how important Greek pottery is as a source of evidence about the Greeks, more because of the paintings on them than what the objects were used for.
▶ Ask the children what the vase shows, and explain the term *hoplite* to them.
▶ Discuss the weapons the Greeks are using.
▶ Point out the characteristic helmet, and explain that these were made of bronze with crests made from horsehair, in the same way as some Roman helmets.
▶ Tell the class what the Greeks usually wore when fighting and discuss who paid for the soldiers' armour.
▶ Discuss the importance of hand-to-hand fighting and explain that Greek youths were trained in these skills from boyhood.

Activities
See 'Frieze', below, for activities on weapons and battle training.

Frieze

This photograph depicts part of a frieze, which was part of the decoration for a mausoleum. Again the influence and significance of warfare in Ancient Greek life is demonstrated. The soldier here is shown only with his shield, or *hoplon*, from which the name *hoplite* was derived. The hoplon was carried on the left arm, leaving the right hand free for the use of weapons. The arm is seen inserted through a strap in the middle of the shield, and the shield can be firmly grasped at the far side with the left hand. The shield would have afforded protection against wounds to the front and left-hand side of the body. When the soldiers moved in their *phalanx* battle formation, however, in closely packed lines, the shield would also have protected the right-hand side of the soldier on their left. Skill in the use of the shield was therefore equally as important as that in the use of weaponry.

Discussing the photograph
▶ Ask the children what this photograph shows. Explain that this is a fragment of a frieze, and discuss the meaning of the word *frieze*.
▶ Talk about what the frieze is made of (marble) and where it is likely to have been placed, for example on a building, probably around the top section.
▶ Tell the class that the shield this fighter is using was called a *hoplon*, from which the name *hoplite* came.
▶ Look closely at how the soldier is using his shield. Discuss how he would only have been able to protect his front and one side of his body.
▶ Explain how skills in using weapons and shields formed a large part of boys' school training.

Activities
▶ Set the children the task of finding names of and details about all the weapons and armour the Ancient Greeks used, and making sketches of these in use. They could then use their sketches to make up a frieze to go around the classroom walls.
▶ Suggest that they work in pairs to investigate all the wars that the Ancient Greeks were involved in. They could then create a simple timeline showing each conflict.
▶ Talk about how the skills needed for fighting on foot were practised in the form of games. Ask the children to list sports and games they know of that could be linked to battle training.

Odysseus' ship on vase

This vase depicts the ship of Odysseus, also known as Ulysses, on his return journey from the Trojan Wars. Depictions of the adventures of Odysseus and the Trojan Wars are extremely common on Greek pottery and highlight the importance of ships and the navy in Ancient Greek warfare. Naval superiority played a significant role in the Athenians acquiring and keeping their empire. This ship is powered by both sail and oars, but unlike the famous *trireme*, this ship only has one bank of oars, and is considerably smaller. The trireme was so called because of the three banks of oars it carried, worked by up to 170 oarsmen. This crew can be seen rowing and operating the tiller, while above them fly three sirens – mythical creatures, half woman, half bird – whose irresistible song lured sailors to their deaths on the rocks. Odysseus has had himself tied to the mast so that he cannot be tempted by the sirens' call.

Discussing the photograph

▶ Ask the children what object is shown in this photograph. Explain that it is the picture on the vase that is of interest, and that many vases like this were made, showing scenes either from everyday life or from myths and legends.

▶ Ask the class if anyone thinks that this scene is from everyday life or perhaps from a myth, and ask them to explain why, for example the sirens.

▶ If they have not heard it before, tell them the story of Odysseus and the sirens, explaining how Greek sailors believed these mythical creatures, half bird, half woman, could really lure them onto the rocks with their singing.

▶ Discuss why Odysseus is tied to the mast, and explain that the other sailors had put wax in their ears so that they would not hear the sirens.

Activities

▶ Talk about the value of the vase as a historical source. Ask the children what they can learn about Greek ships from the picture on it, and to write a brief description from their observations.

▶ Ask the children to find out about Greek ships such as the trireme. Discuss its advantages as a warship, for example speed due to the number of oars and sails; the size of it, which allowed hoplites and archers to be transported for battles, and so on.

▶ Look at the timeline of Ancient Greece (see photocopiable page 30) and ask the children to identify the wars where ships would have been needed.

▶ Ask the children to find out about Greek myths involving ships, such as other stories from the *Odyssey*, and Jason and the Argonauts. Read and perform the play 'Odysseus and the sirens' on photocopiable pages 33–4.

▶ Provide materials for the children, working in groups, to make models or large illustrations of Greek ships.

The Cyclops

The Cyclopes appear in the stories about the adventures of Odysseus attributed to Homer. Giant, mythical creatures, with only one eye, the Cyclopes were the sons of Gaea and Uranus, two of the gods of the Ancient Greeks. In this particular story, the Cyclopes lived alone on an island, dwelling in caves and eating what they could find. Searching for fresh supplies on his homeward journey from the Trojan Wars, Odysseus meets Polyphemus, the Cyclops who he eventually blinds in his one eye and tricks in order to escape death. In this illustration, Polyphemus is shown taller than the nearby trees, fierce and wild, an evil character for Odysseus to triumph over.

Discussing the picture

▶ Look at the picture of the Cyclops and ask if any of the children know what it shows.

▶ Ask if anyone has heard of the Cyclopes and explain that this is an artist's impression of one. Tell the children what the Cyclopes were and how this image is possibly like the one encountered in the stories of Odysseus.

▶ Discuss what is distinctive about this mythical creature, for example one eye, giant in size, ferocious and so on.

▶ Discuss what the Cyclops wears.

▶ Talk about his weapon and his general manner, and consider how he might deal with people he met.

Activities
▶ Tell the children that the story of Odysseus' adventures was written by Homer at around 700BC. Help the children to place this on the timeline of Ancient Greece (see photocopiable page 30).
▶ Explain that the incident with the Cyclops is another of the adventures of Odysseus, on the same voyage as his encounter with the sirens – see page 11. Tell the story of the Cyclops (see photocopiable page 31), or read it with the class.
▶ Provide art materials for the children to design their own mythical beasts.
▶ Challenge them to write a new story about their own mythical creature. They could use Odysseus as their hero or invent a modern hero.

The Minotaur

The Minotaur was a mythical creature with a man's body and the head of a bull. King Minos of Crete had built a special maze in which the Minotaur lived, hidden at its centre. King Minos arranged for young men and women from Athens to be regularly sacrificed to the flesh-eating Minotaur. They would be sent into the labyrinth where they would wander hopelessly lost until the Minotaur found and devoured them. This continued for many years until the Minotaur met with a young man called Theseus, who was anxious to prove himself. He had heard about the plight of seven young men and seven young women who were to be sent to the labyrinth, and so Theseus arranged to go as one of them and protect them, swearing that they would all return safely. Armed with his sword, Theseus entered the labyrinth, found and killed the Minotaur. The illustration here shows the frightening figure of the Minotaur, with bulls' horns, hair and tail, yet with the legs and arms of a man.

Discussing the picture
▶ Look at the picture and ask if anyone knows the name of this creature. Explain that it was known as the Minotaur. Discuss whether it was likely to have ever really existed or whether it was a mythical, invented creature.
▶ Look closely at the illustration and note the special characteristics of the Minotaur – that is, half bull, half man.
▶ Discuss the dangers of meeting a creature like this; ask what it might do.
▶ Explain briefly some of its characteristics and outline the story of Theseus.

Activities
▶ Explain that the Minotaur is taken from the stories about Theseus, a hero from Ancient Greek times. Ask if anyone has heard the story before and encourage them to retell it in their own words. Read through the story of the Minotaur (see photocopiable page 32), and discuss any new vocabulary, such as *labyrinth, maze*.
▶ Encourage the children to discuss how they might have dealt with the Minotaur had they met it, as Theseus did.
▶ Challenge the class to find out about other Ancient Greek myths and to rewrite these in their own words. Make them into a class anthology.
▶ Provide art materials for the children to draw or paint their impression of Theseus fighting the Minotaur. Suggest that they use their knowledge of Greek weapons to help them with their picture of Theseus (see 'Battle scene on vase' and 'Frieze' provided on the CD).

Zeus

Gods and goddesses played an important part in all aspects of Greek life. Ancient Greeks believed in a whole collection, or pantheon, of gods, just as many other early civilisations did. The principal family of gods and goddesses lived on Mount Olympus. These included Zeus, Hera, Hestia, Demeter, Ares, Hephaestus, Aphrodite, Artemis, Apollo, Athena, Hermes and Dionysus. Each god had their own personal history and special influence, which meant that mortals often claimed an affinity with certain gods or called upon particular ones depending on their need. Zeus was the god of both gods and men. He was considered the most powerful of all the gods in both Ancient Greece and Rome, where he was known as Jupiter. His father was Kronos, and he was married to his sister, Hera. Zeus had many children, including Apollo, Athena and Persephone. One of Zeus's great assets was his ability to change himself into numerous different forms and take on the appearance of other people.

Hera

Hera was known as the protector of marriage and of married women. She was said to be the most beautiful of the Olympians and was known by the Romans as Juno. Hera had four children by Zeus and also a daughter named Ilithyia, who was the goddess of childbirth. The stories about Hera are mostly about her jealousy of Zeus and his lovers, and her attempts to punish them and their children. Like Zeus, Hera was believed to send storms, clouds, thunder and lightning, and later on she became queen of the gods and of men.

Discussing the pictures
▶ Ask the children if they have heard of either of these names before, especially Zeus.
▶ Discuss what kind of characters they were and their importance in the hierarchy of gods.
▶ Talk about the powers of these two gods.
▶ Talk about how the Ancient Greeks believed in a *pantheon* of gods.
▶ Notice that the two gods are shown dressed in the style of the Ancient Greeks. Talk about why this was, and what we can learn from the illustrations.

Activities
▶ Divide the class into groups to find out about other Ancient Greek gods. Ask them to find out how many there were and some information about each one. Compile a class book.
▶ Challenge the children to work in pairs to select a story about one of the gods and to rewrite it in the form of a short play. Some of the plays could then be performed by groups.
▶ Suggest that the children create fictitious gods with their own modern powers, illustrating their ideas with stories and drawings.

Model of Temple of Zeus

This photograph shows a model of what the Temple of Zeus at Olympia (see the photograph of the ruins on the CD and the notes on page 17) is thought to have looked like. The temple was a monumental structure and the largest in the Peloponnese. It was built in the traditional Doric style between about 470 and 456BC, and is still highly regarded for the perfection of its style and the high quality of its workmanship. The temple itself consisted of one long room, built to house a massive statue of its god. Surrounding the temple, and supporting the roof, there was an impressive colonnade of symmetrical columns, six on each short side of the rectangle, including the corners, and eleven more on each of the long sides. The structure stood on a base of layered platforms, which also formed steps up to the temple.

Initially designed rather like a simple house, from wood and with a thatched roof, these temples became increasingly elaborate over time. As the Greek Empire grew richer, temples were built from marble rather than wood, and the roofs would be tiled. Carvings and friezes would have been added to enhance the grandeur of the buildings.

British Museum

This photograph shows the facade of the British Museum in London. This is only one of many public buildings around the world to have been built in the Greek style. Often this classical style of architecture was adopted to impress and demonstrate the power and prestige of governments. The colonnade and the stepped platform on which the building stands both resemble the temples of Greece. The figures depicted in the triangular frieze above the middle colonnade reflect the figures in the collection of Elgin Marbles, controversially removed from the ruins of the Parthenon by Lord Elgin, and now kept in the museum. This classical style of architecture may be seen as one of the major legacies of Ancient Greece to modern civilisations.

Discussing the photographs
▶ Ask the children what they think the first photograph shows.
▶ Ask what the tall pillars are called that form the colonnade around the outside (columns).
▶ Ask what they think the inside of the temple may have been like. (One very long room with a high ceiling.)
▶ Explain how the roof was supported and that this gave even more height.
▶ Tell the class how these temples became large and were made with expensive building materials, such as marble, as Greece grew richer.

■ Explain the 'classical' proportions of Greek temples (see photocopiable page 35).
■ Look at the second photograph – the front of the British Museum – and note the similarities with the Greek temple.

Activities
▶ Ask the children to explain in their own words why they think that temples were built to gods such as Zeus, for example to honour him, to make offerings and sacrifices in worship of him. Get them to compare this practice with the use of churches, mosques, synagogues today, and consider what changes have taken place.
▶ Using the knowledge they have about the proportions and style of classic Greek temples, the children could work in small groups to make their own models.
▶ Compare the Temple of Zeus with the British Museum and discuss the legacy of Ancient Greek architectural styles in the modern world. Ask the children to think of other buildings they have seen built in this style and suggest they search on the Internet and in books for other examples. Once they have completed their search, mark on a map of the world all the places they have found where these buildings exist.

Temple of Poseidon

This modern photograph shows the remains of the Temple of Poseidon near Athens. Poseidon was Zeus's brother and the god of the sea, frequently shown in mosaics and statues with his trident. Poseidon was known as Neptune in Roman times. This temple would have been built to house his statue, a place where worshippers would come to make offerings and sacrifices. Here we can see the base of the temple and the columns that would have supported the long sides of the roof. This temple would have been built in the simple, yet elegant Doric style, and despite the ravages of time and looters, the imposing nature of the temple is still apparent from its few remaining parts.

Discussing the photograph
▶ Ask the children what they think this photograph shows. Explain that this is what remains of the Temple of Poseidon.
▶ Discuss why there are only remains of this building. For example, it has decayed over time, weather and earthquakes have damaged it, looters have taken stones for their own use.
▶ Talk about how it still looks imposing even though so much has been lost.
▶ Ask if anyone knows which god Poseidon was; have they heard this name before? Explain that he was the god of the sea.
▶ Talk about why Poseidon was important to the Ancient Greek. Consider the importance of ships in warfare, trade and fishing and discuss why a temple was built to him.

Activities
See 'The Parthenon', below, for activities on both buildings.

The Parthenon

The Parthenon is perhaps the most famous of all Greek temples. Built between about 449 and 432BC, the Parthenon epitomises the classical style of Greek Doric architecture characterised here by rather sturdy plain columns. The tops of the columns were without ornament of any kind and finished with a flat rectangular slab. The Doric style was the earliest, developed in mainland Greece itself, and other variations based upon it were developed in other parts of the Ancient Greek Empire.

The Parthenon was built on the Acropolis in Athens, the highest place in the town (*polis*), to house a huge new statue of the goddess Athena, who had been worshipped in the same place for over a thousand years before this temple was built. Athena was the patron goddess of Athens and a warrior. The colonnade is the main part which still survives, although some of this has been looted, no doubt for the marble and building materials, or removed to museums in other parts of the world. An intricately designed frieze, made to fit into the triangular apex of the front of this colonnade, was removed by Lord Elgin in 1901 and taken to the British Museum in London, where it has become known as the Elgin Marbles.

The stones of the Parthenon are held together not with mortar, but with iron clamps which fitted into carefully designed holes in neighbouring stones. This building technique produced

a seamless, elegant finish. The tall, graceful columns of the colonnades were designed to achieve a similar effect, being held together with plugs of cypress wood fixed into the centre of each section of the column. A major fear for the remains of the Parthenon in modern times is that of pollution, which is gradually destroying the stones.

Discussing the photograph

▶ Ask if any of the class recognises this famous place. If not tell them that it is the Parthenon, built for the goddess Athena.
▶ Explain that it is a historic or archaeological site.
▶ Tell them where it is situated. Ask if the children can work out why this temple was built in such a place.
▶ Discuss why it looks in such a ruined state.
▶ Tell the children about the activities of Lord Elgin (see also the notes on the British Museum on page 13). Explain that the Elgin Marbles are still a cause of friction between the Greek and British governments.
▶ Discuss why Lord Elgin may have removed the stones, and why the museum still refuses to return them.

Activities

▶ Look at a map of Athens and locate the Acropolis, the highest place in the town, where the Parthenon stands. Try to locate the Parthenon.
▶ Compare the Parthenon with the front of the British Museum building (provided on the CD), and note the similarities.
▶ Ask the children to research the three major styles of column that were used in buildings like this – Doric, Ionic and Corinthian.
▶ Divide the class into two and put the children into role, half supporting the views of the British Museum, and half supporting the Greek government, which has asked for the Elgin Marbles to be returned to Greece. Ask one child from each side to prepare an opening speech, and then set up a class debate about the issue, concluding with a vote to decide which argument has won.
▶ Read the text 'Greek temples' on photocopiable page 35.
▶ Encourage the children to use the other photographs on the CD and their knowledge of Greek temples to create their own painting of the Parthenon as it would have looked when newly built.

The Erechtheum

This photograph shows part of the remains of the Erechtheum, which stands on the Acropolis in Athens. It was built in about 420–405BC near to the recently completed Parthenon, principally to house the cult deities of the Athenian state. It was built in the Ionic style, and is unique in the way it was designed to accommodate the needs of many different cults and the graves of the Athenians' ancestors. The steep and irregular slope of the Acropolis was used to good effect in that four different levels, containing three separate temples, were created to house the shrines of each different cult. The statues of draped women shown here are known as caryatids. They have been skilfully used as supports for part of one of the roofs, and at the same time illustrate the type of costume worn by girls at the time.

Discussing the photograph

▶ Discuss what the photograph shows: part of a ruined building.
▶ Talk about the kind of building it was.
▶ Explain to the children that it was built near to the Parthenon on the Acropolis in Athens. Explain that the temple is famous partly because of the way it is built on the side of a steep hill, on four different levels.
▶ Ask the children about the figures – establish that they are young girls. Point out how the figures are cleverly used to support the roof of the porch.
▶ Talk about how these statues are a useful historical source, and ask the class what we can learn about the Ancient Greeks from them.
▶ Point out the Ionic columns used on other parts of the temple.
▶ Discuss why these important buildings were all on this site, for example because it was considered the most important part of the town, being the highest part.

Activities

▶ Find and label the date of the Erechtheum (405BC) on the timeline of Ancient Greece (see photocopiable page 30).
▶ Carry out a search on the Internet with the whole class to find out more about this particular temple.
▶ Look for other pictures of the caryatids, the figures on the building, and ask the children to make their own sketches of them.

The theatre at Delphi

There is known to have been a settlement at Delphi since about 1400BC. However, Delphi became famous throughout the civilised world after about 650BC when the first temple to Apollo was built there. It was the home of the sanctuary of Apollo and the oracle, a designated priestess known as the Pythia, who was believed to be able to foretell the future. This was achieved through her ability to communicate with the god Apollo. The Pythia responded to questions from visitors while in a trance and her cries were then interpreted by an official interpreter and written down. Visitors would travel to Delphi to consult the oracle from all over the Mediterranean region, despite the fact that the responses to their questions were often obscure and ambiguous. Delphi gradually grew in religious and political importance and began to claim to be the centre of the Greek world.

Further up the hillside from the temple of Apollo was the stadium and theatre where the great Pythian festival, an annual event, was held. Despite continual plundering since Roman times, much of the splendour of Delphi can still be appreciated, particularly in this theatre. The sanctuary and oracle had been closed down with the spread of Christianity in Roman times, probably resulting in the theatre and stadium also falling into disuse. These were only rediscovered and excavated in modern times, in about 1893.

Discussing the photograph

▶ Ask the children what the building in this photograph might have been, taking into account its shape and size.
▶ Ask if anyone has ever seen anything similar, or has perhaps been to Delphi.
▶ Discuss the purposes of the theatre, for example to show plays and performances; to hold these in honour of the god Apollo.
▶ Discuss where the audience would have sat and where the players would have given their performances.
▶ Ask the class why they think this building is so well preserved when the others they have looked at have been so ruined, including that it was only excavated just over 100 years ago.
▶ Tell the class about the importance of Delphi as the home of the Oracle.

Activities

▶ Place the date of the building of the temple to Apollo at Delphi (c650BC) on the timeline of Ancient Greece (see photocopiable page 30).
▶ Ask the children to imagine what it must have been like to be in the audience in the theatre at Delphi; to think about the atmosphere, the scenery the sounds. Then set them the task of writing a description of a visit to the theatre in their own words, from the perspective of a member of the audience.
▶ Ask the children to work in pairs to produce advertisements for the theatre, using a variety of art materials.

Olympia

Olympia is located in the western Peloponnese, in a valley between two rivers. It was both an ancient sanctuary and also the site of the ancient Olympic Games, which were held in honour of Zeus, the first one taking place in 776BC. The games lasted for seven days and were held every four years. The Altis was an area containing religious buildings and temples. Outside this area were the priests' houses, baths, guest houses and accommodation for the athletes. This photograph shows the remains of one of the houses specially built for important foreign guests and officials. It is known as the Leonidaion, and was built in 330BC. Only the base of the structure now remains, but the layout of the house can be clearly seen, and it is evident that it was a house of substantial proportions.

lympia stadium entrance

This photograph shows what remains of the entrance to the stadium at Olympia. Originally, this was a long, vaulted passageway through which the athletes would pass into the arena. They would arrive here from special quarters of their own, and would enter the sunlit, crowded stadium from this passageway, similar in some respects to those leading into the later Roman amphitheatres and modern football grounds.

Temple of Zeus at Olympia

This temple, dedicated to Zeus, was built between about 470 and 456BC. It was Doric in style and stood on the southern part of the Altis. The temple was very imposing, partly because of its sheer size, but also because of the stone columns and the carved figures it contained. (See 'Model of Temple of Zeus' on the CD and the notes on page 13.) The enormous statue of Zeus, which it contained, stood over 12 metres high and was clad in gold and ivory. It featured Zeus seated on a throne, holding his sceptre in his left hand and the goddess Nike (representing victory) resting in his right. On his head he wore a sculptured wreath of olive sprays. This statue was considered one of the seven wonders of the ancient world. The branches of the wild olive tree which grew next to the temple were used to make the wreaths for the winning athletes.

Racetrack at Olympia

The racetrack made up part of the stadium at Olympia. It dates from the 5th century BC and is about 212 metres long. On one side of the stadium, there was a stone platform on which the judges sat. 45 000 spectators could be accommodated inside the stadium – however, these places were reserved exclusively for men. Inside the stadium and in other parts of Olympia, there were altars to various deities, and the athletes would be sworn in at the altar of Zeus before the start of the games.

Vase showing athletes

This Ancient Greek vase shows athletes in a running race. Both short-distance races and, later on, races of about two miles were run at the ancient Olympic Games. Other sports that took place include wrestling, boxing, jumping, javelin, discus, horse riding and chariot racing. Ancient Greece was the only ancient civilisation where it is known that sport and athletics were practised and so highly regarded. Indeed, the word *athlete* is derived from Greek. The Ancient Greeks took their sports very seriously, and physical fitness was considered essential for all young men (women did not participate or spectate). It is thought by some historians that the games originated as part of the preparation of young men for warfare, since many of the sports had direct relevance to the type of fighting which took place in ancient times.

Discussing the photographs

▶ Look at the four images of different parts of the site at Olympia and ask the children to identify what they think each picture shows.

▶ Talk about how the full site contained many different buildings, of various functions, as well as the facilities for the games themselves. Explain that these photographs show just a few of them.

▶ Look at the guest house for foreign visitors ('Olympia'). Discuss the size of the building, shown by the remaining foundations of the walls. Talk about its unusual shape.

▶ Discuss the entrance to the stadium and how it was used. Compare it to the modern footballers' tunnel.

▶ Look at the remains of the Temple of Zeus, and discuss why it was at the site of the Olympic Games. Consider the size of the temple, judging from the remains.

▶ Look closely at the picture of the racetrack and explain its length. Mention that the athletes had to be sworn in before they began, in the temple or at altars on the site, suggesting that the games had a religious significance as well as a sporting one.

▶ Finally, look at the athletes on the vase. Compare the runners with modern athletes, and discuss the other reasons young men trained to run fast, sometimes over great distances – to carry news of war and so on.

Activities
▶ Ask for volunteers to recall and place the date of the first Olympic Games (776BC) on a class timeline of Ancient Greece.

▶ Divide the class into small groups and ask them to research, using library resources and the Internet, further information about Olympia: the site, the games and what kind of sporting events took place. Ask each group to collaborate to produce a poster presenting all the information found.

▶ Help the children to find information on the modern games and compare similarities and differences with the ancient games. Complete a piece of shared writing which summarises the points.

Discus thrower in Ancient Greece

This plate decoration shows the ancient art of throwing the discus. Not only was this an important skill to develop for military purposes in the time of the Ancient Greeks, but it also became a highly prized contest in the Olympic Games. The discus was considered a 'heavy' sport unlike the running of a short race, and a separate prize was awarded to the winner of this particular event. The discus itself looks much larger than its modern equivalent and was made from metal, but it appears to have been held and thrown in much the same way. The attendant appears to be in charge of ensuring that each contestant did not overstep the mark when taking his turn.

Modern discus thrower

This modern discus thrower looks, on the surface, quite different from his ancient counterpart. He wears brightly coloured clothes, specially designed for sport, and the discus itself looks smaller than the one shown in the hand of the ancient discus thrower. It is also made of different materials. The enclosure is sealed off from the spectators with netting to avoid accidents and there are sensors to monitor that the athlete remains within the allotted space while releasing the discus. Yet despite all these changes, the essential features of the sport remain the same.

Discussing the photographs
▶ Ask what the picture on the plate shows; discuss what sport is taking place.

▶ Ask what the children think the role of the man in the foreground is.

▶ Consider whether such a stance is actually possible, or whether the artist was more interested in creating a pleasing symmetrical design than an accurate representation of discus throwing.

▶ Ask why and how the throwing of the discus became part of the Olympic Games.

▶ Discuss the importance attached to fitness and to the skills of combat in Ancient Greece.

▶ Talk about why the discus is still used today – how it has become accepted as a sport in its own right.

Activities
▶ Compare the ancient and modern discus throwers and list the similarities and differences with the whole class.

▶ Ask the children to make notes on why the modern discus thrower has to stand inside a sealed-off area; consider changes in attitudes towards safety and why these attitudes have changed.

▶ Provide a wide range of resources for the children to search for further information about the discus – how it was used, whether its use has changed in the modern games, and so on. If possible, provide a real discus for the children to look at in the classroom.

Ancient Greek coin

This coin shows an Ancient Greek javelin thrower. The javelin, like running, was considered an important but 'light' event, and it was awarded a special separate prize. Of course, this sport had great importance in its application to warfare and the training of young men to be competent fighters. The javelin thrower here is depicted inside a marked out area, very much the same as is used in modern athletics, to ensure fairness in comparing the distance of throws.

Modern javelin thrower

The modern javelin thrower uses very similar movements and techniques as his ancient counterpart. Arms and legs are spaced for support and balance and to permit the longest possible throw. What has changed over time is the design and material of the thrower's clothes, and of the javelin itself. Also, of course, the modern javelin thrower takes part in the activity simply as a sport, whereas in ancient times javelin throwing, like the pentathlon, would have been essential training for warfare.

Discussing the photographs

▶ Discuss why the throwing of the javelin became so important in Ancient Greece, for example the link with warfare; training for fitness; as a sport.

▶ Compare these reasons with modern day reasons.

▶ Encourage the children to think about the significance of having a picture of this sport on a coin, comparing it with the images we have on coins and banknotes today. Look at some coins and notes, including from other currencies if possible, to find what and whose images are on them.

▶ Look at the actions of throwing the javelin in the two pictures and discuss whether the movements appear to have changed significantly over the thousands of years between the two.

Activities

▶ Ask the children to write in their own words about the similarities and differences between ancient and modern javelin throwers.

▶ Provide a wide range of resources for the children to search for further information about the javelin – how it was used in both the games and in wars, whether its use has changed in the modern games, and so on. If possible, provide video clips showing the throwing of the javelin in the modern Olympics.

▶ Get the children to mime the movements of a javelin thrower, and while working in pairs, challenge each child's partner to make a drawing which shows the movement of the thrower. Then, help the children to make prints and moulds of the drawings to decorate paper plates or create model coins.

An Ancient Greek school

Not everyone went to school in Ancient Greece. Parents had to pay for their child's schooling, so school was only for the wealthy and was also only considered necessary for boys. Boys began school when they were about six or seven. They were taught how to read, write and count, and how to sing, dance and recite poetry. Children were expected to memorise long stories and poems, sometimes learning the whole of the *Iliad* and the *Odyssey* by heart. Lessons lasted all morning, and in the afternoon a boy was expected to work at his physical fitness. Sports were considered important and boys were encouraged to train and do strenuous exercises. Sports included running, wrestling, boxing, jumping and throwing the javelin and discus. One of the greatest achievements for a young Greek man was to be chosen to represent his city at the Olympic Games.

In Ancient Greece, schooling was principally aimed at training boys for manhood, in manners, morals and physique. The development of a strong moral outlook was considered the most important feature of the training of boys for full citizenship and participation in the democratic process.

Discussing the picture

▶ Discuss what the illustration shows.

▶ Ask for volunteers to point out the different lessons that are taking place.

▶ Ask if the children can see things that are still used in schools today.

▶ Now ask them to point out things that they do not recognise.

▶ Compare the scroll of writing being used by the teacher with the *tablets* being used by the children and discuss why they used different materials for writing.

▶ Note how there are only boys in the school.

▶ Explain how the Ancient Greek school day was timetabled.

▶ Discuss what was considered particularly important in a boy's education in Ancient Greece.

Activities

▶ Compare the activities in this classroom with the activities the children would expect to see in a modern classroom. Ask the children to make notes on the discussion for future use.

▶ Ask the children to list all the things that are specific to schools in Ancient Greece that they can see in the illustration. Add any new vocabulary to the class word bank.

▶ Ask the children to write a story about a day in the life of a schoolboy in Ancient Greece.

The use of the stylus

The Greeks had learned from the Egyptians how to make paper from a plant called papyrus. However, it was considered too expensive to waste on schoolchildren. Instead, children learned, like Roman children later, to write on pieces of wood coated with wax. They scratched letters into the wax using a sharp tool called a stylus. When the lesson was finished the wax would be warmed, rubbed smooth and used again. This 19th-century drawing was published in 1872 in a book called *The Art Journal*. This book was intended to show different epochs throughout history and this illustration demonstrates how important a part writing and study played in Ancient Greek times. The illustration shows the various ways in which the artist believed the stylus was used in Ancient Greece. It can be seen being used on a large wax tablet, in books and on a scroll of paper.

Discussing the picture

▶ Look closely at this picture and discuss when the children think the picture was made.

▶ Ask what they think it shows and why they think it was made, for example to show the different uses of the stylus, to show historical importance.

▶ Explain that the Ancient Greeks developed a form of writing on clay or wax tablets, using an iron implement called a stylus.

▶ Get the children to identify all the different ways shown of writing with the stylus.

▶ Talk about the different writing materials that the Ancient Greeks had, and about who was allowed to use them, using the picture for reference.

▶ Discuss whether it would have been easy to learn to use the stylus.

Activities

▶ Provide some soft 'tablets' of Plasticine, clay or wax and some pointed implements for the children to experiment with writing like the Ancient Greeks.

▶ Help the children to use the Greek alphabet to learn to write some Greek characters and words.

▶ Create some 'scrolls' for them to write on in Greek.

▶ Provide reference materials for the children to make further enquiries about the stylus and its uses. If possible, provide an example of some Greek writing made with a stylus.

Pythagoras

Pythagoras, who lived between 570 and 500BC was a Greek philosopher. He had a deep interest in mathematics, and this interest led him to set up a school in Croton in Calabria. This school made important discoveries and innovations in the field of mathematics. Pythagoras and his students and colleagues believed that everything could be related to mathematics. They agreed that 'all is number'. Pythagoras is famous for his theories about sound, but especially for his work on geometry. Pythagoras' theory is still used in schools today to teach about the lengths of the sides of a right-angled triangle. He was also the first to classify numbers as odd and even, prime and so on.

Socrates

Socrates lived between 470 and 399BC. He was a philosopher in Ancient Greece, who worked hard to raise questions about ethics and virtue in Greek society, and what these meant. His methods of questioning were scientific in their approach and he was well known for his skill in exposing ignorance and conceit. He spent a great deal of his time in the marketplace in Athens, where he liked to converse with the townspeople. However, he became greatly disliked by some because of his views and methods. At the age of 70 he was convicted of treason and corruption of the young and was sentenced to death. He was given a deadly

potion of hemlock to drink and although he had the opportunity to escape death, his belief in the law led him to choose death. Plato, one of his students, wrote about his death.

Plato

This photograph shows a bust of the Ancient Greek philosopher, Plato. Plato lived between 429 and 324BC and founded the Academy in Athens. This was a school in which many important scientific discoveries were made. Plato played an important part in introducing a more rigorous approach to the study of mathematics, although he made no significant discoveries himself. Believing in absolute truth, Plato believed that it was through mathematics that absolute truth could be achieved. Plato is also considered to be the inventor of philosophical argument.

Discussing the photographs
▶ Compare the photographs of the three statues of Pythagoras, Socrates and Plato and discuss their similarities.
▶ Consider the period of time between Pythagoras and Plato, and consider how little fashions had changed. Encourage the children to think about how quickly fashions change in modern times and how slowly they must have changed long ago. Discuss possible reasons why this was, for example communication was difficult and slow; fashion was not considered so important; it was thought to be important to keep up old traditions, and so on.
▶ Discuss the kinds of subjects that all three scholars were interested in and famous for, for example mathematics and science.
▶ Consider how the same line of thought was passed down from one to the other, eventually influencing Greek society.

Activities
▶ Ask for volunteers to label the dates of the three scholars on a class timeline of Ancient Greece.
▶ Read their biographies with the class and get the children to make brief notes about the reasons for the fame of each of them. Suggest that the children use their notes to write a short account of why they are still remembered today.
▶ Ask the children why they think Socrates was executed, and why he did not try to save himself.
▶ Ask the children if they have heard of any modern scholars who will be remembered in the future – Marx, Einstein, Darwin and so on.
▶ Explain how an early version of democracy was developed in Athens during the 6th century BC. Write a list of the different categories in Greek society and ask the children which ones they think would have been allowed to vote in the democracy they had. Discuss whether this would comply with modern notions of democracy.

NOTES ON THE PHOTOCOPIABLE PAGES

Word and sentence cards

PAGES 25–9

The word and sentence cards build on those suggested in the QCA units on Ancient Greece and Greek ideas, and a number of specific types of vocabulary have been introduced, including words related to:
▶ the Ancient Greeks, such as *empire, city state, democracy, slaves*
▶ the Greek language, such as *alphabet, technology, athlete* (and appropriate prefixes and suffixes derived from Greek)
▶ warfare, such as *enemies, hoplite, armour*
▶ Ancient Greek architecture, such as *column, frieze, sculpture*.
Encourage the children to think of other words to add to those provided, in order to build up a word bank for the theme of Ancient Greece and Greek ideas. They could also use the cards in displays, in matching activities and to help them in writing captions for their pictures.
    The sentence cards suggest ways of using the key words to summarise knowledge about the period.

Activities

▶ Once you have made copies of the word cards, cut them out and laminate them. Use them as often as possible in displays or for word games.

▶ Add the words to the class word bank, and encourage the children to use them in their own writing.

▶ Make groups of words that include prefixes and suffixes derived from Ancient Greek and add these to the class word bank.

▶ Encourage the children to summarise their learning at the end of the project and to compose sentences using the key words to help them with their summaries.

Ancient Greeks timeline PAGE 30

This timeline can be used to introduce children to the notion of chronology over a very long period of time, including the long period of Minoan rule over Greece. It uses BC and AD and shows the lives of some of the key Greek scholars. As can be seen, most of the necessary information lies within a fairly short span of time – between about 800 and 100BC. Spans of time have been shown to the right of the line, and key events and the approximate births of the scholars are shown on the left of it.

This timeline could be used alongside pictures of the scholars, and in teaching about the Olympic Games, Alexander the Great, the Battle of Marathon and Athenian rule. It will give children some visual representation of the great length of time during which Greece was an important power. It could be adapted for the classroom in the form of a wall frieze or a long string which could be stretched across the classroom, to represent the distance in time covered by the period. Pictures and dates could be added as the topic progresses.

The kind of timeline shown here can also be useful at the end of a topic for checking children's success in grasping ideas of sequence, chronology and, for those at that stage, understanding of the use of dates. This could be carried out by asking them to create their own version of the timeline, or by giving them a blank outline to complete by positioning events in the correct order and pictures in the appropriate places.

Discussing the timeline

▶ At the beginning of the topic, ask the children what they think this timeline shows.

▶ Clarify what the dates given on the timeline mean.

▶ Look at the 'reading direction' of the timeline. Explain that this represents the passing of time.

▶ Talk about key events and personalities during the period and add more labels as appropriate.

▶ Use the images and biographies of the scholars (see the CD and photocopiable pages 36–8) and the pictures of places provided on the CD to illustrate the discussion about the timeline.

Activities

▶ Make a class timeline, using photocopiable page 30. Ask the children to put on any other pictures or statues from the period they find, in the appropriate places on the timeline.

▶ Suggest the children find other timelines in the class collection of books about Ancient Greece and use these to develop and add to the class timeline.

▶ Give the children a blank timeline with some key dates included and ask them to complete it. This will provide some useful assessment evidence.

Stories of the Cyclops and the Minotaur PAGES 31–2

The story of the Cyclops is a famous Greek myth, but with a background of the Trojan Wars – real conflicts fought in very early times. The stories associated with the wars were passed on by word of mouth and embellished, no doubt over the centuries. The clever play on words will need to be discussed and explained by the children themselves, to ensure they have understood it. The story needs to be told within the context of the adventures of Odysseus on his return from the Trojan Wars as a hero.

Similarly, there are numerous stories about Theseus, another popular figure in the tradition of the hero, who has this exploit among many others in the course of his wanderings.

The children will enjoy hearing about the Minotaur and other strange mythological beasts from this time, and there are also useful links that can be made with literacy.

Discussing the stories

▶ Read the two stories, and ask the children what kind of stories they think they are, for example myths and legends. Ask if they have ever heard these stories before, or any others from Ancient Greece.

▶ Discuss why the Ancient Greeks enjoyed myths, and why they were important to them. Explain how legends are slightly different, since they are based on an event or person that was real. Explain that there were Trojan Wars, although clearly the story of the Cyclops cannot be real. Discuss whether it is a myth or a legend.

▶ Talk about the story of the Cyclops and the use of wordplay – the way in which the words *no man* eventually lead to the downfall of the Cyclops.

▶ Talk about the story of the Minotaur, and ask if anyone has been in a maze. Discuss how a maze works.

▶ Encourage the children to recall the clever way in which Theseus was able to escape from the maze.

▶ Ask them if they know of any modern stories that are based on this idea, for example the film *The Labyrinth*.

▶ Discuss which of the two stories they preferred and why.

Activities

▶ Challenge the children to find other versions of these stories. Ask them to work in pairs or small groups to compare their different versions and to decide by voting which they think is the best.

▶ Provide other stories from the *Odyssey* and ask the children to read them. They can then write some myths of their own, and draw some more mythical creatures.

▶ Look at modern stories with mythical creatures, such as *Where the Wild Things Are* by Maurice Sendak (Red Fox), *The Hobbit* or *The Lord of the Rings* by JRR Tolkien (HarperCollins). Set up a discussion in small groups to identify reasons why myths have been so popular down the ages.

Odysseus and the sirens PAGES 33–4

The children will need to have heard the story of the sirens before attempting to read or perform this playscript. It would be helpful if they have read or heard some of the other stories about Odysseus, so that they understand the purpose of his journey and the significance of the episode with the sirens.

The playscript does not challenge the children heavily in terms of the reading level it requires. However, it will be important to get the children to understand how it works, and especially how the 'chorus' needs to vary the intensity of their sounds at different points in the scene.

Activities

▶ Tell the story of the sirens, and others from the *Odyssey*, to the class.

▶ Encourage the children to rehearse sections of the play in groups, for example as the chorus.

▶ Provide ideas and materials for the children to make scenery and props – oars from stiff card; the side of the ship; waves from fabric, and so on.

Greek temples PAGE 35

This description provides greater detail about Greek temples. It can be used alongside corresponding images on the CD (see 'Model of Temple of Zeus', 'Temple of Poseidon', 'The Parthenon', 'The Erechtheum' and 'Temple of Zeus at Olympia'). The description indicates some of the characteristic features of these buildings and those based on them which have been built in modern times, and will complement any work on this style of architecture.

Discussing the text

▶ Read the description of Ancient Greek temples, and ask for volunteers to give some of the temples' key characteristics.

▶ Ask the children how they might recognise Ancient Greek styles of architecture.

▶ Discuss the words *Doric* and *Ionian*, and explain why features of Greek temples were given these names.

▶ Ask the children what effect the Greek architects were trying to achieve, for example smooth, elegant lines, and the impression of very tall sleek, imposing buildings.

Activities
▶ Use the description in conjunction with the corresponding images on the CD (see above). Encourage the children to select specific buildings on the Acropolis or a particular Greek temple to write their own description.
▶ Challenge the children to search for further information about Greek architects, Pericles (who was responsible for the buildings on the Acropolis), and so on. Make a class book or reference entries on the computer with the information found.

Biographies of Ancient Greek scholars   PAGES 36–8

These brief biographies tell us a little about the time when each scholar was alive, their travels, their interests and their achievements. What is interesting is how similar many of their lives were, involving considerable travel, learning from scholars in other countries, and the widespread interest among them in mathematics. It becomes clear how learning was passed on down the generations from one scholar to another. Some of the passages are quite challenging for primary children to read, and support may be needed, particularly with explaining some of the vocabulary.

Discussing the texts
▶ Read each short biography and explain to the children that these are all scholars from Ancient Greece.
▶ Ask the children whether they have heard any of these names before and if they know what they are famous for.
▶ Compare the dates when they were alive and note the period of time covered by their discoveries and work.
▶ Ask the children what the key things are that they have learned from the biographies.
▶ Ask what kind of information they do not provide.

Activities
▶ Use the timeline of Ancient Greece (see photocopiable page 30) to locate each famous scholar and help the children to make a chart, listing them in chronological order.
▶ Challenge the children to find names of other scholars and add them to their chart.
▶ Make a class book about famous scholars, beginning with those from Ancient Greece and adding more examples from other societies. Set the children the task of also finding out about modern day scholars who are famous, such as Stephen Hawking.

Ancient Greeks word cards

city state

empire

democracy

government

slaves

citizen

legacy

civilisation

Modern civilisation in the West owes much to the legacy of Ancient Greece.

Greek language word cards

alphabet

technology

history

geography

telephone

athlete

Modern words, such as 'technology' and 'telephone', are derived from Ancient Greek words.

Warfare word cards

enemies
hoplite
armour
weapons
tactics
Persian
Marathon
Warfare was very common in Ancient Greece and many young men were trained to be hoplites.

Greek architecture word cards

sculpture
column
frieze
capital
temple
theatre
Parthenon
stadium
gymnasium
Classical Greek architecture has been very popular as a modern building style..

◣ SCHOLASTIC
PHOTOCOPIABLE

Prefixes and suffixes cards

semi...	**photo...**
...racy	**philo...**
...oid	**demo...**
...scope	**pro...**
...logy	**micro...**

Ancient Greeks timeline

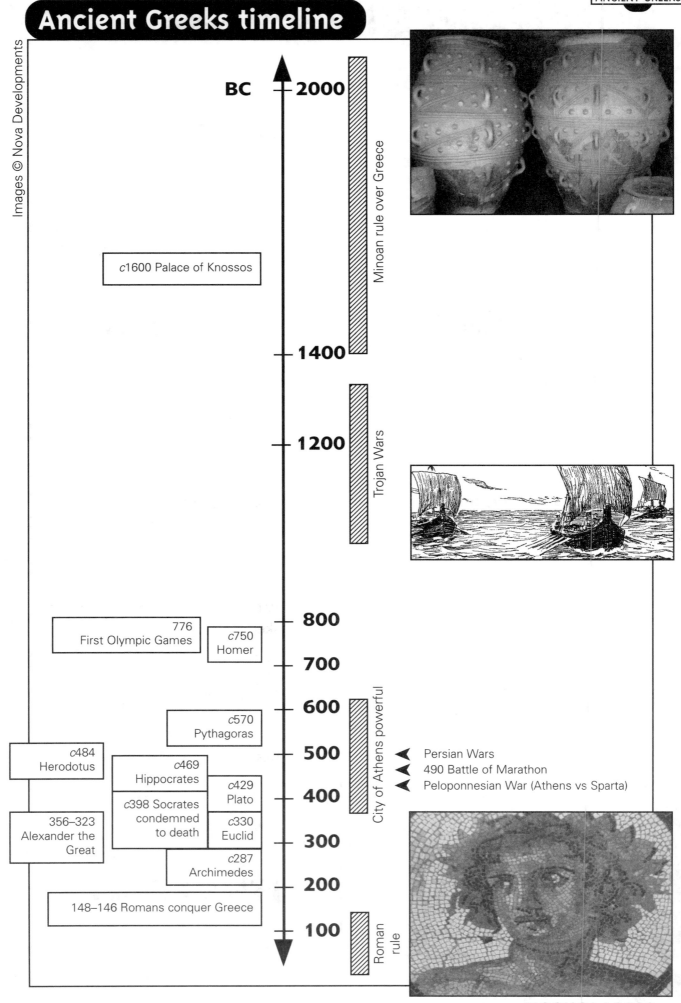

BC — **2000**

Minoan rule over Greece

c1600 Palace of Knossos

— **1400**

Trojan Wars

— **1200**

— **800**

776
First Olympic Games

c750
Homer

— **700**

City of Athens powerful

— **600**

c570
Pythagoras

c484
Herodotus

— **500**

◄ Persian Wars

c469
Hippocrates

◄ 490 Battle of Marathon

c429
Plato

◄ Peloponnesian War (Athens vs Sparta)

— **400**

c398 Socrates
condemned
to death

c330
Euclid

356–323
Alexander the
Great

— **300**

c287
Archimedes

— **200**

148–146 Romans conquer Greece

— **100**

Roman
rule

■ SCHOLASTIC
PHOTOCOPIABLE

Story of the Cyclops

ailing home after his battles in the Trojan War, Odysseus arrived one day at the country of the Cyclopes. The Cyclopes inhabited an island by themselves, and lived off what they could find. They were huge, fierce creatures with great appetites, who would eat anything or anyone that crossed their path. An unusual thing about them was the fact they had only one large eye, right in the middle of their foreheads.

Odysseus and his companions were nearly out of supplies, so they decided to go ashore to collect fresh food. They took a jar of wine with them as a gift for the Cyclopes. They soon arrived at a cave, but found no one inside. Just as they had seated themselves, the owner of the cave, the Cyclops Polyphemus, arrived. After driving in his sheep and goats to be milked, he sealed the entrance to the cave with a huge rock that would be impossible for any number of men to move. Looking round the cave with his huge eye, he soon made out the strangers and demanded who they were. Odysseus explained and very humbly offered the gift they had brought, but Polyphemus reached out and grabbed two men. He smashed out their brains against the wall of the cave and proceeded to devour them. He then went to sleep for the night.

The next day, the giant seized two more of Odysseus' companions and devoured them in the same way. He then left the cave, rolling back the huge rock after him, and went on his day's work.

While he was away, Odysseus planned how he might avenge his murdered friends and escape from this terrifying place. First, he and his companions sharpened a bar of wood and hid it under some straw. When Polyphemus returned he ate two more of the men, but Odysseus bravely went out to speak to him, taking a bowl of wine. The giant enjoyed the wine and asked for more and more. Presently he became more agreeable and asked Odysseus his name.

"My name is No-man," replied Odysseus.

Soon the giant fell asleep, and Odysseus and his companions held the end of the stake in the fire till it was burning hot. They then plunged it deep into the giant's eye, upon which Polyphemus leapt up bellowing in pain and calling out to the other Cyclopes. They gathered outside his cave, asking what had happened.

Polyphemus replied, "Oh my friends, No-man has harmed me."

"What?" they said. "If no man has harmed you, then you must put up with it," and they all went away.

Next morning, the Cyclops rolled away the rock, but instead of going to tend his sheep, he waited to catch the men, feeling each animal as it passed out through the entrance to the cave. Odysseus was ready for him. He told his companions to tie themselves underneath three sheep all tied together, so that they would be hidden beneath the belly of the middle one. Sure enough, the Cyclops felt each sheep as it passed, but did not think to feel beneath it, and in this way Odysseus and his men managed to escape and return to their ship.

Story of the Minotaur

The Minotaur was born, to everyone's horror, with the body of a human, but the head of a bull. When he heard the news, Minos, King of Crete, sent a messenger to the Oracle at Delphi to discover what he should do with this terrifying beast. The Oracle answered that he should build a suitable cage for it, so Minos ordered the construction of the labyrinth, a huge, complicated maze. He placed the Minotaur in the very centre of the labyrinth. King Minos also arranged for young men and women to be sacrificed every nine years to the flesh-eating Minotaur. They would be shut in the labyrinth where they would wander hopelessly lost until the Minotaur found and devoured them.

Meanwhile, Theseus, the son of King Aegeus, was born. When he was old enough, his mother took him to a large rock to see if he could lift it. Theseus was able to do so, and beneath it he found a sword and a pair of sandals left for him by Aegeus, whom he had never seen. The sword was to play an important part in the many adventures Theseus then had.

While on his travels in Athens, Theseus one day saw the preparations being made for seven young men and seven young women to be sent to the labyrinth of the Minotaur in Crete. Theseus was so moved at the sight of this that he immediately swore to save them. He would sail with them and make sure they all returned safely home.

Minos himself came to the harbour when he heard of their arrival, challenging Theseus to prove who he was. As Theseus did so, he was seen by the daughter of Minos, Ariadne, who fell instantly in love with him. Ariadne knew the ways of the Minotaur and the labyrinth, since she had seen so many perish. She suggested that Theseus take into the labyrinth a magic ball of string to help him trace his way in and out. She also gave him a sacred sword, which would help him on his mission.

With these things to help him, Theseus set off into the labyrinth alone, encouraged by the good wishes of the youths and maidens. He wandered for a long time, sometimes coming back to the length of string that he had laid, and having to retrace his steps into a different turning. All the time Theseus could hear the angry roaring and bellowing of the Minotaur, which was by now becoming hungry for its next meal.

Eventually, Theseus turned a corner in the maze, only to see that he had indeed arrived at its centre. Turning swiftly round, Theseus saw, towering over him, the fearsome head of the Minotaur, swaying, and dribbling from its mouth in anticipation of a tasty meal. At last the brave Theseus had a chance to use the sword given to him by Ariadne. He swung it accurately and, with a single blow, severed the head of the Minotaur, saving the young men and maidens of Athens from a terrible fate.

Odysseus and the sirens

Cast:

Narrator	Siren 1	Noctones (helmsman)
Odysseus	Siren 2	Oarsman 1
Chorus	Siren 3	Oarsman 2

CHORUS: Per… Splash… Per… Splash… Per… Splash.

NARRATOR: The oars slice lightly through the still blue waters. Odysseus and his companions are on their way home after the Battle of Troy. They have had many adventures already: they have met the Cyclops, the witch Circe, Odysseus has been to Hades. But now the sun is very hot and it is hard work pulling the heavy ship through the water.

CHORUS: Per… Splash… Per… Splash… Per… Splash.

NARRATOR: To get home they must pass the rocks where the sirens live. Circe has warned them about the sirens – large creatures, half bird, half woman – who sing to sailors and entice them towards the sharp rocks. No sailors who have heard the sirens and followed their calls have ever returned. All have been dashed to death on the rocks and drowned. But Odysseus is ready for them.

CHORUS: Per… Splash… Per… Splash… Per… Splash.

ODYSSEUS: Oh I can hear them now. What strange, wonderful sounds they make. They are the most beautiful sounds I have ever heard in my whole life.

CHORUS: *(softly)* Oooooooooooo! Eeeeeeeeooooooo! Eeeeeeeeeeeeeooooooo!

OARSMAN 1: What is he saying?

OARSMAN 2: I don't hear you. This beeswax we have stuffed in our ears is working well. I can't hear a thing!

CHORUS: Per… Splash… Per… Splash… Per… Splash.

NOCTONES: I can see them now. There they sit on that rock as sharp as glass. There would be no hope if we went near that! This is like a dream. I have never seen such horrible creatures. They are like hideous birds from a nightmare! Just look at those claws and those thick, heavy eagles' legs. Ugh, their skin is green and slimy!

CHORUS: *(slightly louder)* Oooooooooooo! Eeeeeeeeooooo! Eeeeeeeeooooooo!

NOCTONES: What stumpy ugly wigs – they look as if their arms have been cut off at the elbows. I can see their bony faces now with their sharp evil beaks wide open. Oh, help us!

CHORUS: *(louder)* Oooooooooooo! Eeeeeeeeooooo! Eeeeeeeeooooooo!

NARRATOR: The sturdy oarsmen cannot hear the sirens' song, nor can they see them. The helmsman can see their ugly forms, but he cannot hear them either, because they have all stuffed their ears with wax. Only Odysseus can both see and hear them, but he has asked to be tied to the mast until they are safely out of sight and sound of the sirens.

Odysseus and the sirens (cont)

ODYSSEUS: What enchanting sounds. Noctones, please untie me so that I can speak more easily to these wondrous creatures.

SIREN 1: Hear us, Odysseus. We know you have come far to join us.

CHORUS: Per… Splash… Per… Splash… Per… Splash.
(Louder) Oooooooooooo! Eeeeeeeeooooo! Eeeeeeeeoooooooo!

ODYSSEUS: Just look at their lovely smiles and hear their melody. Noctones, you know you must obey my orders. Untie me at once!

SIREN 2: Odysseus, we love you. We will die if you do not come to us.

CHORUS: *(loudly)* Oooooooooooo! Eeeeeeeeooooo! Eeeeeeeeoooooooo!

NARRATOR: Odysseus struggles more and more to free himself from the ropes.

NOCTONES: *(speaking as if to himself)* No one hears the song of the sirens and lives!

ODYSSEUS: *(struggling very hard)* You will never hear the last of this Noctones unless you let me go! I will kill you if you don't untie me!

CHORUS: *(more softly)* Oooooooooooo! Eeeeeeeeooooo! Eeeeeeeeoooooooo!

SIREN 3: Odysseus, why are you leaving us alone on this rock? Come back, come back.

Odysseus struggles harder still, but cannot untie the ropes.

CHORUS: Per… Splash… Per… Splash… Per… Splash.

(Very softly) Oooooooooooo! Eeeeeeeeooooo! Eeeeeeeeoooooooo! Per… Splash… Per… Splash… Per… Splash. *(Now very faintly)* Oooooooooooo! Eeeeeeeeooooo! Eeeeeeeeoooooooo

NARRATOR: Odysseus finally stops struggling to free himself. He is exhausted, but happy to be past the rocks. They row on without a word for some time.

NOCTONES: Put up your oars and rest. I said PUT UP YOUR OARS AND REST!

OARSMAN 1: What? Did he say something?

OARSMAN 2: I can't hear nothing. Me ears is still full of that wax. Let's clear it out. Ah that's better.

NOCTONES: Put up your oars.

OARSMAN 1: Thank goodness, let's have a rest.

NOCTONES: I think we all need one. I'm glad I didn't hear them things though. You should have seen them, ugly things! You should have seen how Odysseus struggled to get at 'em! Let's untie him now, I think we're safe.

Noctones and Oarsman 2 untie Odysseus.

ODYSSEUS: *(sounding relieved)* What an experience! I want to get as far away from this place as I can. Ah! I can feel wind on my face. Let's haul up the sail and head for home. Row as well, men, and we can make better time.

© Jon Lingard-Lane
www.ziptheatre.co.uk

Greek temples

The temples of Ancient Greece were built for the worship of gods and making offerings to them. Each temple would be dedicated to a specific god, such as Zeus, Athena or Apollo, and his or her statue would be placed inside it.

Originally, the temples would have been wooden structures, built in the shape of a house, with a thatched roof. There was a single room and a small front porch supported by wooden columns. Over time, the temples became increasingly elaborate and more expensively designed and constructed. As the Greek Empire grew richer, they were built from marble rather than wood, and the roofs were tiled. A colonnade of large marble columns was added, which ran around the outside of the building. The columns supported the roof, but also created a most impressive and imposing exterior and entrance to the temple. Gradually, the length of the temple was increased to make the approach to the shrine longer and more awe-inspiring. Carvings and friezes were made from marble instead of wood to enhance the grandeur of the buildings. These were used to decorate the 'entablature', the part of the building between the tops of the columns and the roof.

The two styles of temple most characteristic of classical Greek designs were the Doric and the Ionian. The traditional Doric style featured severe geometric designs, and developed on the Greek mainland. The Ionic style grew up in the Greek city states that were founded in Ionia (modern Turkey). These temples featured more elaborate columns and a continuous frieze sculpted in relief around the upper part of the entablature.

The length and width of the temples conformed to specific proportions considered to be the most elegant. The stones were fitted together without mortar, instead using metal bolts that could not be seen from the outside. This meant very precise shaping of each piece so that the finished effect appeared seamless. This was especially important for the columns, which were joined by plugs of cypress wood running trough the centre of each block. The overall effect was one of smooth, uninterrupted lines, designed with harmony and symmetry.

Greek architects did not like to make changes in their designs except to refine and perfect traditional forms. As they grew more skilled, Greek builders began to introduce refinements to create optical illusions that enhanced the graceful appearance of these large temples. For example, they made the columns taper slightly towards the top to make them appear taller. They also made them slant inward to enhance the illusion of great height. These building techniques were so successful that they have been copied around the world ever since.

Photograph © Nova Developments

Biographies of Ancient Greek scholars

Pythagoras

Pythagoras was a philosopher and mathematician who became one of the most famous scholars in world history. He was born in about 570BC on the island of Samos, and probably had a Greek mother. He died in about 500BC. Little is known about his childhood, but he is known to have travelled in the Greek colonies, and was taught by the mathematician, Thales, who advised him to continue his studies in Egypt. Pythagoras managed to carry this out, although political changes made his plans difficult at times. Egyptian scholars were highly proficient in mathematics at that time and Pythagoras learned much from them. However, further warfare led to his capture and removal to Babylon, where once again his abilities were recognised and he was given further instruction from the priesthood in mathematics, geometry and music.

In 522BC, Pythagoras was able to return to Samos, where he set up a school known as the Semicircle. The people of Samos, however, wanted Pythagoras to act on their behalf as a politician and diplomat. Unhappy with these new roles, he left Samos. In 518, he arrived in 'Greater Greece', which was then in Italy. He based himself in Kroton, on the 'heel' of modern Italy, and founded a school dedicated to the study of mathematics and philosophy.

The Pythagorean school regarded geometry as the highest form of mathematics, and its students believed that everything depended upon mathematics. Pythagoras was interested in the close relationship between mathematics and music. He was the first to prove the accuracy of the theory that the square of the hypotenuse on a triangle is equal to the sum of the squares of the other two sides. The Pythagorean view of the world was to greatly influence another famous philosopher and mathematician of the Ancient Greek world, Plato.

Archimedes

Archimedes lived between about 287 and 212BC. He was a famous mathematician and engineer in Ancient Greece, and made important contributions to our knowledge of geometry. He discovered how the lever works and is reported as saying, "Give me a lever and I can move the world."

His most famous discovery was apparently made while he was in his bath. He realised that the volume of water displaced by an object immersed in water is the same as the volume of the object itself. This is known as

Biographies of Ancient Greek scholars (cont)

Archimedes' principle. Archimedes is reputed to have run through the streets when he discovered this principle, shouting "Eureka!" (I have found it).

It is also thought by some that Archimedes invented and designed new war machines for Greece, including catapults, cranes and giant curved mirrors for training the sun's rays and burning approaching foreign warships.

Euclid

Euclid lived from around 330 to 275BC, and is known as one of the most significant of the Ancient Greek mathematicians. He is best known for his work on geometry, and one whole part of our knowledge of geometry is known as Euclidian geometry. Very little is known about how he grew up or how he spent his life, but it is thought that he studied at the academy of Plato in Athens.

Most writing about him suggests that he was a kind, fair and very patient teacher, helping his pupils with their work and also encouraging them by pointing out that even kings have to study hard to learn geometry.

Euclid wrote 13 books called *Elements*, and these are some of the world's most famous books. They laid down the basic knowledge needed for the study of almost all geometry, and became the most important geometry textbooks for hundreds of years. The first and possibly most important of the books explains points, lines, planes, angles, circles, triangles, quadrilaterals and parallel lines. *Elements* was translated into Latin and Arabic, and is one of the earliest known books to survive to the present day, almost two and a half thousand years later. Because of this work on geometry, Euclid is known as the 'father of geometry'.

Herodotus

Herodotus was a historian in Ancient Greece and is sometimes called the 'father of history'. He is thought to have lived between 484 and 425BC, and is believed to have travelled widely in Asia, Babylon, Egypt and Greece. These travels must have given him a good knowledge of most of the important parts of the region at that time.

In about 447, he is thought to have travelled to Athens. Here he soon became known and won the praise of many scholars and important leaders,

Biographies of Ancient Greek scholars (cont)

such as Pericles. In 443, he went to live in southern Italy, which was then a Greek colony, and he stayed there for the rest of his life, writing *The Histories*.

The Histories has been divided into nine parts, and is thought to be, on the whole, one of the most reliable sources of ancient history. It is also famous for the excellent quality of Herodotus' writing. The first books tell us about the customs, legends, traditions and history of those people in the ancient world known to Herodotus. The last three books are about the wars between the Persians and the Greeks in the fifth century BC, where Herodotus presents Greece and Persia as the two centres of eastern and western culture.

Hippocrates

Hippocrates is one of the earliest doctors we know of. Living between about 469 and 399BC, he lived on the island of Kos and studied medicine, becoming one of the most famous physicians and philosophers of the ancient world. Like many other scholars of his time, he travelled widely and studied hard. Eventually he became known as the founder of the *science* of medicine, separating it from religion or magic. He spent most of his life working in his medical school on Kos, but also offered his skills and knowledge of medicine to many other cities in Ancient Greece. In 430BC he was invited to Athens by Pericles, and helped to save the people from a deadly plague. To honour him, the Athenians made him a citizen of Athens, also granting the same rights to the other inhabitants of Kos.

Hippocrates made some astonishing observations that are still valuable to us today. His principles were set out in a work known as *Aphorisms*, which was regarded as one of the key books about medicine for hundreds of years. Hippocrates was also the inventor of the 'Code of medical ethics', in which he set out the duties of doctors and rules about how they should treat their patients.

After his death, a sanctuary for the sick was built on Kos. It was dedicated to the Greek god of medicine, Asclepius. It was built in a place thought to have a healthy climate and good water. It became very famous throughout Greece and the sick travelled great distances to it in search of cures for their illnesses. It was an early type of hospital.

INDUS VALLEY

Content, skills and concepts

This chapter on the Indus Valley relates to unit 16 of the QCA Scheme of Work for history at Key Stage 2. This unit deals with a non-European civilisation and aims to demonstrate how archaeologists have worked to recreate an account of a civilisation from the distant past using limited evidence. It also shows how interpretations of historical evidence can differ greatly. Together with the Indus Valley Resource Gallery on the CD, this chapter introduces a range of sources, including photographs of archaeological sites and artefacts, archaeologists, maps, reports, descriptions and accounts. These can be used in teaching about the Indus Valley as an ancient civilisation on a par with Greece and Egypt. The chapter also provides materials to support the teaching of key historical concepts relevant to this period and theme.

Children will have gained experience, while working on other history units, of sequencing and using timelines, using time-related vocabulary, asking and answering questions, and using visual, written and auditory sources. Recounting stories about the past, and looking for similarities and differences between the past and the present, are learning activities which will have introduced relevant skills and concepts to the children before they progress to the skills and concepts in this unit. The chapter includes suggestions for extending these and other skills, such as recognising change and continuity and selecting information to support an argument, for example about the interpretation of archaeological sources.

Resources on the CD-ROM

A map, plan of Mohenjo-Daro, photographs of the site and of objects found in the Indus Valley, photographs of the archaeologists and some of the excavations are provided on the CD. Teacher's notes containing background information about these sources are provided in this chapter, along with ideas for further work on them.

Photocopiable pages

Photocopiable resources are provided within the book and in PDF format on the CD from which they can be printed. They include:
- ▶ word and sentence cards
- ▶ a timeline
- ▶ accounts
- ▶ extracts.

Teacher's notes are provided in this chapter to accompany all the photocopiable text resources. They include suggestions for developing discussion about the pages and for ways of using them for whole class, group or individual activities.

History skills

Skills such as observation, description, the use of time-related vocabulary, sequencing, use of a timeline, understanding the meaning of dates including BC and AD, comparing, inferring, listening, speaking, reading, writing and drawing are involved in the activities provided. For example, there is an opportunity to develop independent skills in source analysis through close investigation of some of the artefacts discovered at Harappa and Mohenjo-Daro. Children can learn to use descriptive vocabulary to describe the maps, pictures, illustrations and photographs included on the CD.

Historical understanding

In the course of the suggested tasks, a further aim is for children to develop a more detailed knowledge of the past and to sequence and date events independently, through their understanding of the context and content of the factual information they use. They will begin to give reasons for events, use sources to find further information and be able to recount and rewrite stories and accounts they have heard, sometimes using different forms of presentation. They will also have the opportunity to extend their skills in using descriptive language and specific time-related terms to write their own factual accounts of the past. Communication skills of various types can also be practised and developed.

NOTES ON THE CD-ROM RESOURCES

Indus Valley civilisation

This map shows the location of the Indus Valley – so named because of the River Indus, which stretches from the Himalayas down to the Arabian Sea. An ancient civilisation called the Harrapan Civilisation grew up around the banks of the river between 2600 and 1900/ 1800BC, in much the same way as the Ancient Egyptian civilisation developed in relation to the River Nile. These very early civilisations depended on close proximity to a regular supply of water and on rich farming land, and consequently developed along the banks of large rivers such as the Indus and its tributaries. Approximately 1500 sites have been discovered in an area spanning 1 200 000km² and reaching into three countries – India, Pakistan and Afghanistan. The two largest cities discovered in the Indus Valley are Harappa and Mohenjo-Daro.

Discussing the map

▶ Ask if anyone knows what continent the Indus Valley is to be found in. Look at the map with the whole class. Look at the inset map which sets the larger map in context. Notice that the Indus Valley civilisation spans across three countries.

▶ Look at the more detailed version. Ask someone to find the Himalayas and the River Indus.

▶ Explain that the Indus Valley civilisation developed along the shores of the river and then spread outwards. Point out that archaeologists in recent times think that the same civilisation may have reached far into India.

▶ Point out where sites have been found – in particular Harappa and Mohenjo-Daro. Explain that Mohenjo-Daro is in Pakistan.

▶ Ask if anyone has visited this part of the world and talk about what it is like now.

Activities

▶ Ask if anyone has visited the famous archaeological sites at Mohenjo-Daro or Harappa. Discuss how long ago these ancient cities flourished, and locate the dates on the timeline (see photocopiable page 53).

▶ Give the children labels containing the names of each major period in British history, and ask them to place them on a class timeline. Compare these with the location of the Indus Valley civilisation. Note where there seem to be gaps on the timeline and discuss the reasons for this, for example lack of historical information about those periods.

Sir Mortimer Wheeler

There have been a number of archaeologists who have worked on the sites in the Indus Valley since the 1920s, but one of the most famous is Sir Mortimer Wheeler – shown in this picture. He was the first archaeologist to organise a systematic enquiry into the sites of the Indus Valley civilisation during the 1950s. Here he is shown during his excavation work. He was known for the systematic methods he used of dating objects according to the levels and locations of their discovery. Sir Mortimer Wheeler, in addition to his work as an archaeologist, also published books about his work and popularised the study of archaeology through his television broadcasts about it. He worked with his wife to set up an Institute of Archaeology which still thrives in London. Wheeler published, among others, a book called *The Indus Civilisation* in the 1960s. He worked on Roman archaeological sites in Britain at Verulamium (St Albans) and Maiden Castle as well as carrying out major excavations at Mohenjo-Daro and Harappa. Since these early excavations, many more important ancient settlements have been found in both Pakistan and India.

Discussing the photograph

▶ Look closely at the photograph with the class. Ask if anyone can suggest what the people in it are doing.

▶ Explain and discuss the meaning of the words *archaeologist* and *archaeology*.

▶ Tell the children that this is a photograph of Sir Mortimer Wheeler, who was a well-known archaeologist, at the excavation of the site at Mohenjo-Daro.

▶ Discuss how long ago they think the photograph was taken. (1950s.) Talk about the clues that tell us it is an old photograph, for example Wheeler's suit and hat.

▶ Discuss what Wheeler is doing and consider how important it is for an archaeologist to collect every item that is found.

▶ Talk about what happens to all the artefacts that are discovered, for example they are classified and labelled.

▶ Tell the class that the site has been dug in rectangles in trenches with straight sides. There are strings marking off sections. Discuss why this was done – so that the exact spot where artefacts were found could be marked on a plan of the site.

▶ Explain how the exact depth or level at which they are found is also important. Ask the children if they know why this is, for example because the depth of an object gives a clue about its age, since the deeper objects are in the ground, the older they usually are.

Activities

▶ If possible, find an area in the school grounds and mark out a small square or rectangle. Get the children to draw a plan with grid lines and then mark out the grid lines with string. They can then 'excavate' their site and mark on their plan the things that they find. Challenge them to find a way of showing the different levels that they dig through.

▶ Explain that many Asian archaeologists have worked in this area, both with Sir Mortimer Wheeler and more recently. Provide the children with appropriate resources and set them the task of finding out about some of the other archaeologists who have studied these important sites.

▶ If possible, take the class to visit a real archaeological site, where they can see the whole process in action. There are also some useful broadcasts, such as *Time Team* shown on Channel 4, which the children can watch as an alternative to a visit.

Reconstruction of Mohenjo-Daro

It is thought by archaeologists that the city of Mohenjo-Daro was built about 5000 years ago and that people lived there for six or seven hundred years. There seems to have been a high citadel and a lower town, although only a very small fraction of the city has been excavated so far. In the lower city there are wide streets and narrow lanes, and a mixture of large and small houses. High walls still remain, carefully built from bricks. There were streets of varying widths and Sir Mortimer Wheeler believed that they may have joined up to form a grid. It is possible that the city had been carefully designed and laid out like modern towns. Another idea is that it may have just grown as people kept adding more streets and houses.

This illustration shows an artist's interpretation of what Mohenjo-Daro may have looked like. Historians are able to use archaeological evidence to discover much about Mohenjo-Daro, including the structure and layout of the city, tools that were used, crops that were grown, weapons, weights and measures used and animals that were kept. However, there is still a great deal about the Indus Valley civilisation that remains unknown. For example, their religious beliefs, how the society was structured and why the cities declined and the civilisation ended. In this picture the artist has shown the Indus River running close to Mohenjo-Daro. 3700 years ago the river changed its course and it no longer runs as close to the site. The illustration shows the Citadel (see page 42) and it is also possible to see the 'Great Bath' (see 'Street scene – Mohenjo-Daro' on page 42) with its columned corridor.

Discussing the picture

▶ Look carefully at the illustration and discuss the area it shows.

▶ Ask the children why they think there was a *high citadel* and a *lower city*. Explain that these are names given to the areas by the archaeologists who excavated them.

▶ Discuss who is likely to have lived in each area, for example the ordinary people and workers would have lived in the lower city.

▶ Compare the idea of a grid layout of the streets with modern cities such as New York.

▶ Discuss why we know about some things about Mohenjo-Daro and not others.

Activities

▶ Use the timeline (see photocopiable page 53) to locate the period of the Indus Valley civilisation.

▶ Give the children a blank outline map of this part of the world and help them to label the Indus Valley and some of the cities and sites that have been excavated.

▶ Provide the children with small 'viewfinders' (card rectangles, each with a space to look through). Ask them to place their viewfinder over one interesting section of the picture. They can then write a detailed description of this section.

Street scene — Mohenjo-Daro

Sir Mortimer Wheeler drew up detailed plans of Mohenjo-Daro based on the extensive evidence of streets and houses that were excavated. Some streets were very wide, like modern main streets. For example, the largest street, known as First Street, is 11 metres wide. Other smaller streets, of which there were many, were called lanes by the archaeologists, and some were just one metre wide. Most streets had floors of beaten earth, but some were paved. Many of the streets had drains running beneath them. Because of the very wet environment in this area, the buildings' wooden roof beams have rotted away, but walls, windows and doorways can still be clearly made out.

On the right-hand side of this photograph you can see the 'Great Bath'. It lies in the middle of a large building. It has a smooth paved floor and walls made of brick and a large drain in one corner where the water ran out. A corridor must have run around the bath and there are small bathrooms on one side of the corridor. It is not really known what the bath was used for – it may have been used for bathing or possibly for religious ceremonies, the small bathrooms being used by the priests.

Discussing the photograph

▶ Look at the photograph with the whole class and ask for volunteers to talk about what they can see.

▶ Explain that this is one of the streets at Mohenjo-Daro, with different sorts of buildings on either side.

▶ Discuss what the remains show us – the houses, doorways, rooms, living areas, street layout and so on.

▶ Point out the large structure on the right-hand side of the picture, and ask if anyone can work out what it might have been. Discuss what we can speculate about the 'Great Bath'.

▶ Tell the children that this was part of a large building with corridors and other rooms containing smaller baths.

Activities

▶ Discuss how much of what is thought is simply worked out by archaeologists, and that we do not know for certain. Talk about why we may be correct about the 'Great Bath'. Explain that the walls are lined with a waterproof layer of tar, suggesting it held water. Look at the other clues that suggest it was a bath. Discuss who may have used it and why. Compose a short information passage about the 'Great Bath' as part of a shared writing session.

▶ Encourage the children to find illustrations and pictures of other large public baths, such as Roman ones and modern ones . Look at where these different eras come on the timeline (see photocopiable page 53). Ask them to note the features of the other baths that we know about and compare these features with the 'Great Bath' at Mohenjo-Daro. They can then write an argument as to why they do or do not agree with the archaeologists' interpretation that this was a bath.

▶ Provide art materials for the children to recreate their impression of what the Great Bath might have looked like.

The Citadel at Mohenjo-Daro

Mohenjo-Daro consists of the Citadel and lower city. This photograph shows the Citadel, with the Buddhist Stupa (which dates from about the 1st century AD), in the background. One theory about the Citadel is that the whole area may have been a palace, or it may have been the area where the ruling elite lived, separate from the town where the common people lived. The Citadel once had high walls and towers. However, even larger houses have been found in the lower city, suggesting that maybe there were a number of powerful families, or that there were civic buildings of great importance. On the Citadel, the archaeologists found a number of different buildings, which they named after deciding what they may have been used for. There was a 'Great Bath', the Buddhist Stupa, a 'Great Granary' (since questioned), a college (possibly for priests), a pillared Hall and some fortifications. About 600 wells have been found there so far.

Discussing the photograph

▶ Discuss what can be seen in the photograph, and talk about what these different constructions might have been.

▶ Look up the meaning of the word *citadel*, and talk about why one part of the city was built on high ground.

▶ Look at the tall building in the background, and explain to the children that this was built by Buddhists at a later date. Explain that it is called a *Stupa*, and that it was put on the highest part of the citadel.

▶ Ask what problems for the archaeologists may have been caused by the presence of the Stupa, for example they know there are buildings underneath it but they cannot dig down to them.

▶ Look at the remains of buildings in the foreground and discuss what they might be.

Activities

▶ Compare the 'Reconstruction of Mohenjo-Daro' (provided on the CD) with this photograph and ascertain what these remains are.

▶ Ask the children to look up the word *citadel* on the Internet to find other examples of them around the world. Ask them to record their findings and compare notes on what they have found with a partner.

▶ Discuss the idea of 'interpretation' and how archaeological evidence can be interpreted in different ways. Explain that archaeologists and historians often have differences of opinion on how evidence should be interpreted. Ask the children to research some of the different interpretations archaeologists have had on buildings in Mohenjo-Daro, in particular the Granary, and then write a report of their own about their conclusions.

Well at Mohenjo-Daro

This is a well in a small house off one of the lanes in Mohenjo-Daro. There were many wells like this one throughout the city. Some of them stand like tall chimneys because of the removal of surrounding soil. Near some of them are stone benches, and many broken cups have been found around the wells or in the drains outside.

Discussing the photograph

▶ Look at the photograph of the well with the whole class and discuss its location in relation to the walls of the surrounding buildings.

▶ Discuss how the archaeologists knew what it was.

▶ Talk about why it was made inside the house, when wells that we see in this country are outside, for example this may have been so that people could be out of the Sun's heat as they used it.

▶ Tell the class what was discovered around the well and in the drains outside – broken drinking cups.

▶ Discuss what probably used to happen around the well.

▶ Ask the children to list all the different uses for the well.

▶ Explain to them that several hundred wells have been found in the city, and discuss why so many were needed.

Activities

▶ Look up information about wells together to discover how many different types of wells there are.

▶ Encourage the children to find out about wells and oases in the desert, and about their importance.

▶ Discuss why wells are not used very much in many countries today. Think about those countries where wells are still used. Discuss the problems associated with safety in drinking water.

▶ Make a class book about wells in different parts of the world.

Statue of the Priest-King

This famous statue was found by an archaeologist called Mr Dikshit in 1927 in Mohenjo-Daro. It was found in an unusual house with fancy brickwork and niches in the walls. The buildings in this part of the city were very large and Mr Mackay, another archaeologist who excavated them, thought that some could be palaces. The statue was found broken, lying in the house along with other objects such as animal seals (see page 46). The statue is approximately 18cm high and has traces of red paint on the trefoil design on the robe. The eye sockets appear to have been inlayed, possibly with shell. Gold headbands like the one seen on the statue have been found in other houses and there is also evidence that the statue was further decorated with possibly a necklace. The hair and beard are combed and the hair may have been held in a bun, as is traditional, although no bun has been found.

Discussing the photograph
▶ Ask the children to point out the interesting features of the statue.
▶ Make a note of these on a board or flip chart, including features such as facial features, beard, headband, other jewellery, costume.
▶ Discuss what these features might suggest about the subject of the statue, for example an important person, possibly with a religious role.
▶ Encourage the children to think about the circumstances of its discovery: broken, on the floor. Consider what might have happened and why, for example religious images destroyed by people with different beliefs, or an invading group.

Activities
▶ Talk about the name given to the statue by the archaeologists, and go through the reasons it was chosen, using the list made during the discussion. Decide why each feature does or does not fit the title. Ask the children to work in pairs to write a reasoned argument in favour of this title.
▶ Ask the children to work in pairs to search on the Internet for further information about religion in the Indus Valley civilisation. Ask them to make notes on their findings, then compile all the notes in a shared writing session. Talk about why we don't know much about the religious beliefs at the time.
▶ Look at the details of the statue and talk about whether it may have been a religious symbol. Provide materials such as clay for the children to make their own Priest-King model statues, perhaps making sketches or plans on paper before they begin working in 3-D.

Chariot

This chariot, pulled by two oxen, is similar to several terracotta animals on wheels and toy carts which have been found at Mohenjo-Daro and other sites. This example, probably made of bronze, is very detailed, and it shows how oxen were used to pull carts and vehicles. It also reveals that people in this ancient civilisation had discovered the use of the wheel and had begun to invent technology to meet their needs.

Discussing the photograph
▶ Ask the children to suggest names for the object the photograph shows.
▶ Talk about the features that suggest this was a model or toy version of a chariot that would have been used.
▶ Discuss whether the shaft and fixings on the object look like modern replacements or whether they look the same as the chariot itself.
▶ Talk about why all the parts have lasted, and discuss how this suggests that the whole is made from a metal, probably bronze.
▶ Explain to the children that most items made from anything perishable, such as wood, textiles or leather, have rotted away over time and particularly because of the wet conditions in the area. Conclude that this suggests that if all the parts of the chariot are original, then it must be made of metal.

Activities
▶ Discuss and write about the significance of the discovery and use of the wheel, for example it signalled the development of technology to solve problems.

▶ Ask the children to search for other examples of wheeled objects and toys from the Indus Valley civilisation, using books, the Internet and packs of resources. Ask them to choose one example each and to write about its construction and uses.

▶ Challenge the children to write an imaginative piece about a child who may have been given this toy chariot as a present. Discuss what kind of child this is likely to have been, and what level of society they would have come from.

Bronze figurine

This figure from Mohenjo-Daro is 11 centimetres high, of bronze on a modern stand. She is wearing many bracelets which are seen frequently on other female figurines. In this case she is wearing them mostly on one arm. She also wears a necklace and has an elaborate hairstyle. A curious feature is the hole, just discernible in the photograph, in her left hand. This suggests that the figure may have been used as a stand for an implement of some kind.

Discussing the photograph

▶ Explain to the class that the figure in this photograph is original, but the stand is a modern one, to enable it to be displayed.

▶ Ask the children what they think the figure is made of, and discuss how they know, for example if it had been wooden it would have rotted away.

▶ Note the style of the artwork, and how natural the pose is.

▶ Discuss why the girl may have been portrayed in this way, without clothes. Maybe it was an ornament for a bathroom; perhaps it was not considered problematic to be seen without clothes, like men in Ancient Greece and some tribes today in Africa and South America; perhaps it was fashionable to make figures of nudes, as in art in more recent times.

▶ Note the bangles and necklace; perhaps these were fashionable in the Indus Valley civilisation.

▶ Point out that, although it is hard to make out, there is a hole in the statue's left hand. Ask the children to conjecture why this may have been. For example, could the statue have acted as a stand for some kind of implement or tool, such as a taper to light candles, or some kind of bathroom implement?

Activities

▶ Ask the children to make observational drawings of the statue, perhaps in pastels or charcoal.

▶ Challenge them to write a description of the type of person portrayed in the statue.

▶ Suggest they make a list of all the possible uses the statue might have had.

Weights

Lots of weights like these have been found in Indus cities across the Indus Valley. They were made from stone such as chert (a kind of quartz) and were used in balancing scales. The scales were often made of two copper plates suspended from a stick. The weights would go on one plate and whatever you were weighing would go on the other. The discovery of these objects again suggests an advanced civilisation that used a standardised system of measurement to carefully weigh goods, possibly for sale. It has been suggested that they may also have been used to control trade or collect taxes.

Discussing the photograph

▶ Ask the children what they think these objects are.

▶ Look at the sizes of them, using the ruler in the picture as a rough guide.

▶ Discuss what they are likely to be made of, for example wood would have rotted away. Explain that they are made from stone called chert, and ask why stone was used.

▶ Talk about why there are six carefully graded stones and then one which is much larger. Ask the children if they can understand what this large one was for. (It was a multiple of one of the smaller ones.)

▶ Consider how carefully they are made and talk about why this was, for example to ensure accurate measures of goods; to make sure the measures were fair; perhaps to charge some kind of payment for the goods being weighed.

▶ Discuss how they would have been used, explaining to the children the way hand-held balances can be used.

Activities

▶ Provide a balance for the children to examine to see how it works. Suggest to them that they use some weights with the balance and write some step-by-step instructions for its accurate use.

▶ Challenge the children to work in pairs and make a set of their own weights. They can identify a material that they could use to make weights from, such as Plasticine, wood or clay, and discuss which would be best for the purpose. They could discuss how much they want each weight to weigh and how they would organise the measures within the number of weights they are making.

▶ Talk about the skills of the craftsmen who probably made the weights, and during a shared writing lesson make an inventory of the types of products that could have been weighed in ancient times using weights and scales like the ones discussed.

Jewellery from Mohenjo-Daro

Jewellery like necklaces, headbands, bracelets, bangles, belts and brooches have been found in hoards hidden in houses in the town. As can be seen, much of it was made from gold, copper and precious metals. Beaded work also seems to have been very popular. These were made of different types of coloured stones, joined together using rods of copper. The large object in the photograph is thought to have been a belt because of its size. The discovery of objects of this quality suggests that the civilisation that existed here 5000 years ago was much more advanced than had been previously thought. People obviously had a high standard of living and enjoyed comfortable lives. Small pieces of jewellery have also been found, suggesting that jewellery was also worn by children.

Discussing the photograph

▶ Ask the children what kind of objects these are.

▶ Find volunteers to try to identify each object. For example, a headband is second from the top, with an inverted 'v' shape in the middle; the large item is a belt (worked out from its size). Each of the long beads measures 12 centimetres, so the whole is long enough to fit round a person's waist.

▶ Look closely at the objects and ask the children to work out what the pieces are made from.

▶ Discuss who may have worn them and why.

▶ Note that some of the pieces are very small and this suggests that children also wore jewellery.

▶ Talk about what the artefacts show us about the people of the Indus Valley civilisations, for example that they were fairly affluent; they had skilled craftsmen; they had artistic tastes and skills; they chose colours and materials sensitively; they valued the same sort of precious metals and stones as are valued today.

Activities

▶ Look at the photographs of the two figurines, 'Statue of the Priest-King' and 'Bronze figurine' (provided on the CD), to find examples of jewellery being worn in Mohenjo-Daro. Ask the children to use these photographs in conjunction with this one to draw pictures of the jewellery being worn.

▶ Provide art materials (artstraws, threads, gold paint, and so on) for the children to make their own replica jewellery.

▶ Challenge the children to write an imaginary account about the excitement of an archaeologist on finding one of these pieces of jewellery in the ruins at Harappa.

Stone seal

Stone seals like the one shown in this photograph have been found in numerous quantities in the Indus Valley cities. The pictures and symbols are carved into the stone. This seal shows the very popular image of the one-horned animal. This image appears on most of the seals in the Indus region, along with images of bulls, elephants, rhinos and compositions of various animals. It has not yet been possible to understand much of the Indus Valley script, and so we cannot know what the people of the Indus Valley thought about these various animals and why they were depicted on the seals. Some historians think that the one-horned animal may

have been the sign of the most powerful group of people, possibly traders, in the region. It is likely that there will have been legends about it too. The seal would have been pressed into clay to make a copy, and many pieces of clay stamped with seals have been found in buildings where goods were packed or kept. This suggests that they may have been the mark of the trader who supplied the goods.

Discussing the picture

▶ Explain to the children that this is a picture on a seal, made of stone, that was found in the Indus Valley.

▶ Discuss what seals were for, and tell the class that many have been found in this region and in other parts of the world.

▶ Encourage the children to look closely again at the design of the seal.

▶ Find volunteers to try to identify the images on the seal, such as the one-horned animal, the chalice-like object and the pictograms.

▶ Talk about the one-horned animal, and discuss why such an animal should be represented on many of the seals.

▶ Tell the children that the chalice-like object shown often appears with this animal on other artefacts that have been found.

▶ Look at the pictograms and see if the children can suggest any meanings for them. Tell the class that it has not been possible as yet to decipher the meaning of this ancient script.

Activities

▶ Provide a wide range of sources for the children to find further examples of seals. Suggest they try to group the seals they have found into categories and identify the most popular images on them.

▶ Provide the children with art materials to make their own designs and drawings using the images from the seals. Make a class frieze composed of these designs.

▶ Discuss the purposes of the seals, such as their use when sealing sacks of merchandise. Get the children to devise short dramatic scenes about incidents in the 'packing houses' where the seals were discovered.

NOTES ON THE PHOTOCOPIABLE PAGES

Word and sentence cards
PAGES 51–2

The word and sentence cards build on those suggested in the QCA unit on the Indus Valley, and a number of specific types of vocabulary have been introduced. These include words associated with:

▶ the Indus Valley civilisation, such as *pictograms, ideograms, seal, granary, citadel, kilns*

▶ the passing of time and archaeology, such as *ancient, century, BC, AD, archaeologist, museum, evidence, site, layers, artefact.*

The children should be encouraged to think of other appropriate words to add to those provided, in order to build up an extensive word bank for the theme of the Indus Valley. They could also use the cards in displays, in matching activities and to help them in writing captions for their pictures.

The sentences provide examples of ways in which knowledge about the civilisation that the children have learned can be summarised and new vocabulary incorporated into their writing.

Activities

▶ Add the words to the class word bank, and encourage the children to use them in their own writing.

▶ Encourage the children to summarise their learning at the end of the project and to compose sentences using the key words to help them with their summaries.

▶ Encourage the children to use the word cards to devise their own word games.

▶ Use the sentence cards as examples for the children when writing their own information texts about the topic.

Indus Valley timeline

PAGE 53

This timeline can introduce children to the notion of chronology over a very long period of time. It uses BC and AD and requires them to understand how long periods of time can be shown within an even longer span. The main purpose of the timeline is to show children how long ago the Indus Valley civilisation flourished and how long it lasted in comparison with modern periods. The section showing British history since the Romans is hardly any longer than that of the Indus Valley section.

This timeline could be used alongside photographs of the site and the objects found at Mohenjo-Daro. It will give children some visual representation of the great length of time during which the Indus Valley civilisation occurred. It could be adapted for the classroom in the form of a wall frieze or a long string which could be stretched across the classroom, to represent the distance in time covered by the period. The section on the Indus Valley itself could be used and expanded to show more detail, and pictures and dates could be added as the topic progresses. This more detailed timeline would also be useful at the end of a topic, for checking children's success in grasping ideas of sequence, chronology and understanding of the use of dates.

Discussing the timeline

▶ At the beginning of the topic, ask the children what they think this timeline shows.

▶ Look at the 'reading direction' of the timeline. Explain that this represents the passing of time. Discuss how much time is illustrated in the timeline.

▶ Clarify what the dates and spans on the timeline mean. Discuss the period of the Indus Valley civilisation and why it is shown like this, as part of a longer timeline which also shows British history.

▶ Talk about key events and objects that have been found from the period and add more labels as appropriate.

▶ Use the photographs of Sir Mortimer Wheeler and the pictures of objects and places provided on the CD to illustrate discussion about the timeline.

Activities

▶ Make a class timeline using the timeline on photocopiable page 53. Ask the children to put on any other pictures or photographs from the Indus Valley period they find in the appropriate places on the timeline.

▶ Suggest the children find other timelines in the class collection of books about the Indus Valley and use these to develop and add to the class timeline.

▶ Give the children a blank timeline with some key dates included and ask them to complete it. This will provide some useful assessment evidence.

The Lower City of Mohenjo-Daro

PAGE 54

This text describes the impression of the ancient residential area of Mohenjo-Daro gained by Sir Mortimer Wheeler from his excavations of the site. Wheeler and his team used their own experience upon which to base their theories about this ancient city. The layout of the streets and houses would have been clear to them from the foundations of walls and paving that they found among the ruins. However, more conjecture has been used in describing and identifying the uses of specific buildings. A key example of this is the granary on the Citadel. More recent research has demonstrated the possibility that these theories are, in fact, incorrect, and that buildings like the granary have been incorrectly named. What remains of great interest about the work of Sir Mortimer Wheeler, however, is the revelation that such a highly developed, complex civilisation was flourishing at such an early time in the past.

Discussing the description

▶ Use the 'Reconstruction of Mohenjo-Daro' (provided on the CD) for the children to look at when reading this description. Point out the location of the Citadel.

▶ Find volunteers to show where east would be and to point out the part of Mohenjo-Daro that is being described.

▶ Explain the meaning of *watercourse*.

▶ Look closely at the plan of the streets while reading the second paragraph. Talk about the way in which many modern cities and towns are built on a grid plan, for example New York.

▶ Encourage the children to think about why some streets were built to be very wide and straight.

▶ Discuss why the 'lanes' were narrow and crooked.

▶ Ask the children why Sir Mortimer Wheeler thought the large building was a bath, for example its size and shape. Explain that it was lined with tar and had a large water drain running from one corner (see also 'Street scene – Mohenjo-Daro' provided on the CD).

Activities

▶ Look at the timeline (see photocopiable page 53) and point out when cities like Mohenjo-Daro and Harrapa were built. Ask the children to work out how long ago this was.

▶ Use the pictures 'Reconstruction of Mohenjo-Daro', 'Street scene – Mohenjo-Daro' and 'The Citadel at Mohenjo-Daro' (provided on the CD) for the children to develop their understanding of the city. Ask them to review them, choose one favourite picture and then to write about it.

▶ Provide art materials for the children to create their idea of what this part of Mohenjo-Daro might have looked like.

Archaeologist's report

PAGE 55

This report, by Sir Mortimer Wheeler, shows how difficult the archaeologists' work in the Indus Valley was. Mud, continually washed down by the river, had created layers and layers of coverings over the ancient remains, so that sometimes it was necessary to dig down almost 30 feet to get to them. Additionally, the water level had risen, meaning that some of the lowest, and possibly most interesting early remains, could not be excavated, at least with the equipment available at that time. The work of the archaeologists was further frustrated at times by the fact that over the years, people had moved or used many of the bricks for other purposes, making it even harder to decipher their significance.

Discussing the report

▶ Use the 'Reconstruction of Mohenjo-Daro' (provided on the CD) when discussing this report, and ask for volunteers to point out which part of the city it is about.

▶ Discuss whose report it is. Talk about the work of Sir Mortimer Wheeler and the kind of work done by archaeologists. Ask the children what kinds of difficulties they might experience, and what exciting things they might discover and the adventures they might have.

▶ Look again at the first paragraph of the report. Discuss how the Citadel had been built – high up and with a bank around it. Talk about the reasons for this.

▶ Discuss the meaning of the word *citadel* and ask the children to think about why the archaeologists decided this is what they had found.

▶ Talk about how the discovery of the towers might have contributed to this theory.

▶ Consider the significance of finding 100 hard clay balls above the gate that were found. Consider what the clay balls may have been for and how they were used, for example ammunition for slings.

▶ Ask the children why the archaeologists could not continue further down with their excavations. Talk about why the site filled with water.

Activities

▶ Find the dates of Wheeler's excavation work in the Indus valley and help the children to locate the period of the excavations on the timeline (see photocopiable page 53).

▶ Use the 'Modern world map' (in the Tudor exploration Resource Gallery provided on the CD) to help the children locate the Indus valley, and use a map of the area to find Harrapa and Mohenjo-Daro, using 'Indus Valley civilisation' (provided on the CD) for reference.

▶ Ask the children to describe the work of archaeologists. Discuss the kind of things they need to know, such as the history and geography of the area they are working in, collection and classification methods, methods of dating finds, and so on. Clarify for the children that archaeology attempts to reconstruct the origin, prehistory and the history of the human race using material remains such as artefacts, settlements, earthworks, burials and skeletal remains. It also uses evidence for human impact on the natural environment such as pollen, soil erosion, and animal and plant remains. Challenge the children to write a clear definition of the word *archaeologist*, or alternatively to create an adventure story from the point of view of an archaeologist.

A house at Mohenjo-Daro

PAGE 56

This extract describes in some detail one of the best preserved houses that was found by Wheeler and his team. The layout and uses of the rooms that he describes may seem strange to children and they will benefit from looking at the pictures on the CD ('Reconstruction of Mohenjo-Daro', 'Street scene – Mohenjo-Daro' and 'Well at Mohenjo-Daro') while reading or listening to the text. What is particularly interesting about the houses is the apparent emphasis on water and drainage. The people of the Indus valley seem to have mastered much of the technology necessary for the use of water in many different ways.

This extract from Sir Mortimer Wheeler's book, written for adult, academic readers, may be quite challenging text for some children. However, its focus on the details of a house that was excavated will be a familiar, meaningful topic for them to understand.

Discussing the extract

▶ Ask the children why they think Wheeler picked this particular house to write about.

▶ Ask why there was a well-room in each house, and what this was for.

▶ Consider how the archaeologists decided that one room in this house was a bathroom.

▶ Why did they think there may have been another storey, or upstairs?

▶ What do the children think the archaeologists might have found most surprising in these very ancient houses?

▶ Ask the children what they think the use may have been for the chamber with three niches in the wall. Explain the meaning of *niche*.

Activities

▶ Ask the children if they have ever been to a town in the East. Discuss what the houses are like, and think about why they are built in this way. Get the children to write a list of key features of houses in the Ancient Indus Valley civilisation.

▶ Set the class the task of drawing an interior of a house, based on the reports and writings of Sir Mortimer Wheeler (see also photocopiable page 54) and the images 'Street scene – Mohenjo-Daro' and 'Well at Mohenjo-Daro' (provided on the CD). They could draw the courtyard, the bathroom, the well-room, and so on.

▶ Make a wordsearch using words from the vocabulary list and from the extract, such as *niche, court, well*, and so on.

▶ Challenge the children to write a piece of descriptive verse about life in the Indus Valley.

Indus Valley word cards

pictograms

ideograms

seals

granary

citadel

kilns

The people of the Indus Valley civilisation were beginning to write in a script that used pictograms and ideograms. They put pictograms on the seals that have survived.

Archaeology word cards

ancient	**century**
BC	**AD**
artefact	**museum**
site	**layers**

archaeologist

evidence

Archaeologists now agree that the Indus Valley civilisation seems to have lasted from 2500BC to 1500BC.

Sir Mortimer Wheeler was well known as an archaeologist for the methods he introduced into site excavations.

Indus Valley timeline

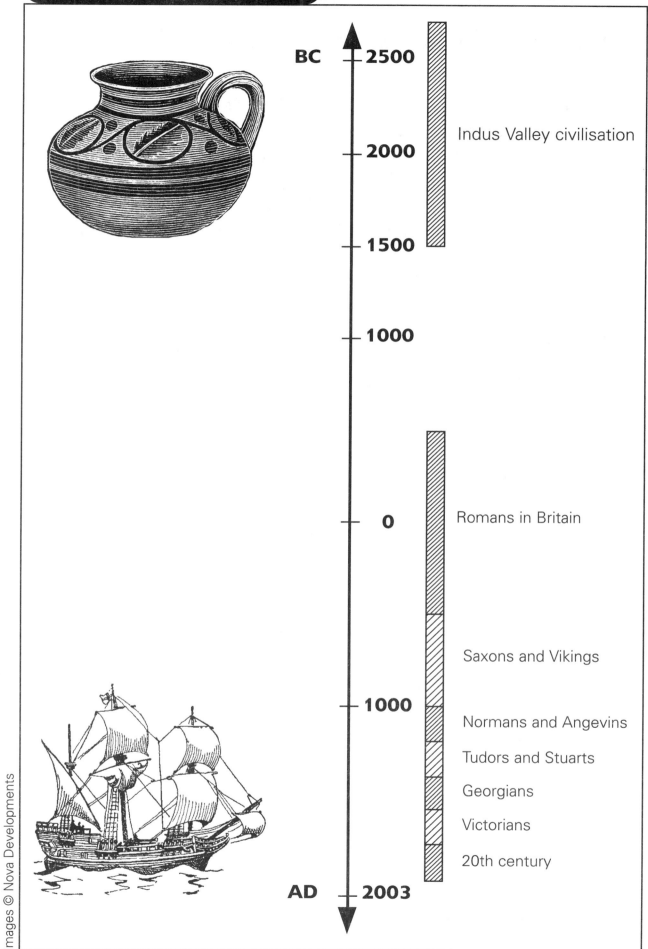

BC

2500

2000 — Indus Valley civilisation

1500

1000

0 — Romans in Britain

Saxons and Vikings

1000 — Normans and Angevins

Tudors and Stuarts

Georgians

Victorians

20th century

AD 2003

The Lower City of Mohenjo-Daro

East of the Citadel of Mohenjo-Daro, archaeologists have found the remains of what Sir Mortimer Wheeler called the 'Lower City'. Between this area and the Citadel, Wheeler thought that there would originally have been a watercourse, either a canal or a branch of the River Indus. Excavations have shown a very large structure along the edge of what may have been a watercourse. They have concluded that this was a large wall built as a flood defence.

The streets in the Lower City appear to have been carefully planned in a grid pattern. The streets run north-south and east-west, dividing the area into rectangular blocks all of a similar size. Excavations have revealed two main streets, which are quite wide and run at right angles to each other. There is also evidence of part of a third main street and of the blocks between them, filled with narrower lanes. The main streets are very wide, approximately 10 metres, while the lanes are only 2 or 3 metres wide. The lanes often have bends or sharp changes of direction – possibly, Wheeler thought, to break up the draughts from the prevailing winds.

The doorways of the houses opened onto these narrow lanes, but there is little evidence of any outward facing windows. The aim of this design appears to have been to avoid direct sunlight and to ensure great privacy. Instead the rooms opened onto an inner courtyard.

In addition to the houses, a large structure that appears to be a large bath has been found in the Lower City of Mohenjo-Daro. It is thought that this may have been used as a communal bath house or maybe for some religious ritual.

◢ SCHOLASTIC
PHOTOCOPIABLE

Archaeologist's report

In places, the team of Sir Mortimer Wheeler had to dig as deep as 10 metres to excavate some of the ruins at Mohenjo-Daro, which looked like two mounds on the Indus plain. They found different periods of building, which they called *early, intermediate* and *late,* or *mature.* They knew, however, that there were even earlier, older ruins beneath the ones they had found, but they could not dig down to them because of the level of the water table.

We dug a section deep into the edge of the mound. The buildings of the Citadel are built on a specially made platform, 6 metres high, of mud and brick. A mud-brick bank 13 metres wide goes round the platform to stop flooding. The platform and the bank were built in the intermediate period.

There are ruins of high walls and towers 9 x 6 metres wide at the south-east corner, with burnt brick foundations. One tower was built at the same time as the platform and more were added later.

We found a bricked-up gate between two towers, with 100 baked clay balls on a wide wall at the top.

There were ruins 7 metres deep below the platform. We cannot find out what they are because when we dug a shaft down, it filled up with water from the water table under the city.

A house at Mohenjo-Daro

A well-preserved house in this area is typical of the general domestic arrangement. Out of a lane 5 feet wide, a doorway opens into an entrance-room or small court, with a tiny porter's lodge on the side facing the doorway. Internally the brickwork was rendered in mud-plaster, of which a portion remains. A short passage, with a small well-room to the south, leads on to the main court, 33 feet square, which was originally open. On the side adjoining the well-room, with which it communicates through a small opening, is a bathroom floored with finely jointed bricks. Under the next room to the east, an earthenware pipe encased in brickwork is carried through from the courtyard to a street drain in the main street. Another earthenware pipe, built vertically into one of the walls, carried drainage from the roof or, as the thickness of the walls would appear to imply, an upper storey, which was reached by a brick staircase in a compartment on the north side of the court. On the west side is a chamber of unknown function with three niches in the northern wall.

In a house of this kind it may be supposed that the focus of activity was the main court. The noteworthy and recurrent features of these houses are the insistence on water supply, bathing and drainage, together with a substantial stairway to the upper floor. In some houses a built seat-latrine of Western type is included on the ground or first floor, with a sloping and sometimes stepped channel through the wall to a pottery receptacle or brick drain in the street outside.

from *The Indus Civilisation* by Sir Mortimer Wheeler, supplementary volume to *The Cambridge History of India*, 3rd edition, 1968, CUP

TUDOR EXPLORATION

Content, skills and concepts

This chapter on Tudor exploration relates to Unit 19 of the QCA Scheme of Work for history at Key Stage 2. This unit deals with the history of early British and European exploration, enabling children to learn about the reasons for, and the results of, world exploration by people in the 16th century. Other explorations as well as those by the Tudors have been included. Together with the Tudor exploration Resource Gallery on the CD, this chapter introduces a range of sources, including maps, illustrations, photographs, portraits, plans, accounts and stories. These can be used in teaching about Tudor and early Spanish exploration and discoveries, as well as introducing children to some aspects of the indigenous populations of America. There are also materials to support the teaching of key historical concepts relevant to this period.

Recounting stories about the past, and looking for similarities and differences between the past and the present are prior learning activities which will have introduced relevant skills and concepts to the children before they progress to the skills and concepts in this unit. This chapter includes suggestions for the extension of these and other skills, such as recognising change and continuity and the ability to select and use information, for example in describing cultures in different parts of the world.

Resources on the CD-ROM

Maps of the world from different times in the past, plans, illustrations, photographs and paintings are provided on the CD. Teacher's notes containing background information about these sources are provided in this chapter, along with ideas for further work on them.

Photocopiable pages

Photocopiable resources are provided within the book and in PDF format on the CD from which they can be printed. They include:
▶ word and sentence cards
▶ a timeline
▶ stories and other texts about life on board ship
▶ attitudes to circumnavigation
▶ accounts of settlement.

Teacher's notes that accompany the photocopiable pages include suggestions for developing discussion about the pages and for using them for whole class, group or individual activities.

History skills

Skills such as observation, description, the use of time-related vocabulary, sequencing, use of a timeline, understanding the meaning of dates, comparing, inferring, listening, speaking, reading, writing and drawing are involved in the activities provided. Children can learn to use descriptive vocabulary to describe the maps, plans, illustrations and photographs provided on the CD.

Historical understanding

In the course of the suggested tasks, a further aim is for children to develop a more detailed knowledge of the past and to sequence and date events independently. They will begin to give reasons for events, use sources to find further information and be able to recount and rewrite stories and accounts they have heard, sometimes using different forms of presentation. They will also have the opportunity to extend their skills in using descriptive language and specific time-related terms in beginning to write their own factual accounts of the past. Communication skills of various types can also be practised.

Photograph © Ingram Publishing

NOTES ON THE CD–ROM RESOURCES

Ptolemy's world map

Ptolemy was a Greek who lived in Alexandria in Egypt between about 87 and 150AD. He was well known as a scholar, specialising in astronomy, mathematics and geography. One of his most famous works, the *Geographia* was the principal geographical text for scholars until the time of Columbus. In fact it was Ptolemy's map of the world, shown here, that Columbus is known to have taken with him on his first voyage to the Americas in 1492.

What is interesting is the extent of scholars' knowledge about the world as early as the first and second centuries AD, and also the fact that they were well aware that the Earth was a sphere. Here we see the surface of a sphere projected onto a flat plane for the first time. The main weakness of the map is that Ptolemy extended the land mass of Asia too far into the east, a factor which some think might have encouraged Columbus to sail west to get to the east.

Tudor world map

This map is by Sebastian Cabot (c1484–1557), a Venetian mariner and explorer who lived in Bristol and made a number of voyages in the early 16th century. Cabot is known for his discovery of Newfoundland in the quest for a north-west passage to the east. It was engraved in 1544 and shows considerable development and greater accuracy in a number of ways compared with the map of Ptolemy, although the basic knowledge of Africa, Asia and Europe remains similar. What is most interesting is the way the continent of America has been placed near the centre of the map. Also the outline shapes of the other major continents that were known of at that time are much more accurately drawn than in the map of Ptolemy. By this time, there had been circumnavigation of the world, and cartographers knew about the southern extensions and shapes of the continents, since they had been travelled around on these early voyages. The map clearly illustrates man's developing knowledge of his world.

Modern world map

By the modern period, almost every part of the world has been explored. We now know the extension of the north and south poles, and Australasia has been discovered and charted in detail. Many of the groups of islands in the Pacific have also been added, particularly the heavily populated islands of Indonesia. Apart from greater accuracy in the position and shape of the major land masses and oceans, there is noticeably greater accuracy on the modern map in terms of the measurements of distances. For example, the Equator and Tropics of Cancer and Capricorn are marked. Most importantly, however, in terms of navigation, the Prime Meridian is marked. This enables sailors to use longitude as well as latitude, enabling the use of a grid to pinpoint the position of a ship at sea – a relatively recent innovation.

Discussing the maps

▶ Look first at each of the three maps separately. Tell the children that the map of Ptolemy was made in ancient times, almost 2000 years ago.

▶ Discuss how long that was before it was used by Columbus.

▶ Think about why such an ancient map was still being consulted in the 15th century.

▶ Find volunteers who will try to identify parts of the world on Ptolemy's map.

▶ Next look at the map made in the 16th century. Explain to the children that this will have been made soon after many of the great explorers had made their voyages of discovery.

▶ Ask for volunteers to point out the areas of the world that they recognise on this map.

▶ Discuss the main differences between this and Ptolemy's map.

▶ Find volunteers who can point out what they think is missing on the Tudor map. Discuss why these things are still missing.

▶ Finally, look at the modern map. Compare this with the earlier maps, and ask the children to point out the areas of the world that have been explored in more recent times.

▶ Compare all three and point out that even in the time of Ptolemy, people obviously knew that the world was a spherical shape. Discuss what the evidence is for this: the map shows a sphere drawn onto a flat plane.

Activities

▶ If possible, provide the children with a copy of a very early medieval 'Mappa Mundi'. These were maps showing the Earth as a flat disc, with Jerusalem at the centre. Tell the class about the belief many years before the time of Columbus that the Earth was organised according to religious belief, and that everything centred on the birthplace of Christ. Ask the children to find out about other versions of the Mappa Mundi, and of people such as Copernicus and Galileo, who challenged this way of thinking.

▶ Challenge the children to research brief histories of the major European explorers, such as John and Sebastian Cabot, Frobisher, Chancellor, Magellan, da Gama, and so on. Ask the children to make brief notes about their findings for future use.

▶ Group the explorers according to their nationalities – Portuguese, Spanish or British – and set the class the task of making a display about each group using their notes. They will need some guidance on display techniques before putting up their work.

▶ Ask the children to write up their observations and discussions about the different maps. Display the maps and writing in chronological order.

Queen Elizabeth I

Although the foundations of the British navy were laid by her ancestors, Henry VII and Henry VIII, Elizabeth's reign saw the greatest expansion in sea travel and exploration up to that time. Under Elizabeth, Drake and Raleigh, among many others, carried out their famous and infamous enterprises, including circumnavigation, discoveries of new lands, piracy, and the establishment of settlements in the 'new world'. This painting, known as the *Armada Portrait*, is a very significant one. It is attributed to George Gower and was painted shortly after the defeat of the Spanish Armada, in 1588 or 1589. It shows the Queen seated in front of paintings of the Spanish Armada which had recently attempted to attack England but had been defeated and effectively destroyed. The Queen rests her hand on a globe of the world in a symbolic gesture indicating to all England's growing global power. A similar portrait of Sir Francis Drake (provided on the CD) was produced at about the same time, showing him also with his hand on the world.

Discussing the portrait

▶ Look at the portrait with the whole class and ask the children what their first impressions are.

▶ Discuss who the portrait shows and what kind of person the portrait suggests she is.

▶ Pick out the key features of the picture, for example the stately robes of the Queen, her hand placed on the globe, the pictures behind her.

▶ Tell the children that the pictures show the Spanish Armada. Ask them if they know what happened, and talk about the victory of the English in this conflict with Spain. Discuss how the picture is a celebration of this victory. Tell the children that this is known as the *Armada Portrait*.

▶ Focus on Elizabeth sitting with her hand on the globe of the world, and discuss what this pose implies. Explain that in Tudor times most ordinary people did not read at all, so information had to be passed on using pictures. Explain how meanings in these pictures were often symbolic. In the case of this portrait, the hand on the globe is telling the viewers that she sees herself as ruler of the world, or at least with power and influence over the world.

Activities

▶ Help the children to locate and label the defeat of the Spanish Armada and the date of the *Armada Portrait* on the timeline (see photocopiable page 76).

▶ Set them the task of researching further into the defeat of the Armada and the role of Francis Drake, making notes on their findings.

▶ Provide suitable art media for the children to make their own Armada pictures, showing different parts of its eventual destruction, such as the burning of the ships by Drake, or the wrecking of others in the storms off the Scottish coasts.

▶ Challenge the children to write an imaginary letter from Queen Elizabeth to the portrait painter, setting out her requirements for the portrait.

Sir Francis Drake

Sir Francis Drake was a favourite of Queen Elizabeth I. This was largely due to his destruction of the power of the Spanish Armada in 1588, and also because of his success as a kind of official pirate. He was knighted following his circumnavigation of the world, which he completed between 1577 and 1580. Drake spent much of his time, however, harassing the Spanish treasure fleets, as they sailed back to Spain from their colonies in South America. These treasure ships were filled with gold, silver, precious stones, expensive dyes, and sugar which was still rare in Europe and highly prized. The precious metals and stones had either been forcibly taken from the indigenous Native Americans, or had been mined in great quantities. They were shipped out of South America, particularly Mexico and Peru, by merchants who traded them for luxury goods sent back from Spain for the Spanish colonists. As these large, heavy fleets progressed across the Atlantic, Drake and comrades such as John Hawkins, would steal up on them, and take the treasure back to Queen Elizabeth. Following one voyage, Drake was able to give the Queen £300 000.

Discussing the portrait

▶ Look at the portrait of Francis Drake and note its key features.
▶ Ask the children what they already know about Drake, and supplement their knowledge where necessary.
▶ Discuss his dress, appearance and the fact that he is leaning on a globe of the world.
▶ Consider the attitudes that people like Drake might have held in the Tudor period. For example, they were very confident of their own prowess.
▶ Discuss what the portrait conveys about the personality of Drake, for example the scarf at his neck may hint at his privateering past; his expression suggests confidence and possibly cunning or arrogance; he looks clever and intelligent; his costume is rich, suggesting he is a wealthy man; he sees himself as an important person in the world.
▶ Ask the children if they think he should be a man remembered as one of the most famous people in history. Did his activities really make him a great man, for example privateering, carrying slaves from Africa to the Caribbean?

Activities

▶ Ask for volunteers to find out about the life of Sir Francis Drake and then label his major exploits on the timeline (see photocopiable page 76).
▶ Find out as much as you can about Sir Francis Drake and his life, and take the 'hot seat' in which you assume the role of Drake and allow the children to ask you questions they have devised themselves.
▶ Ask the children to write a description of Sir Francis Drake, using the comments discussed above about what the portrait tells us of his personality.
▶ Compare the portrait of Drake with 'Queen Elizabeth I' (provided on the CD).

Golden Hind

The *Golden Hind* was the famous ship in which Sir Francis Drake sailed around the world. Built in Plymouth in 1576, it was a galleon, with a wooden hull and armed with 18 guns. It needed a crew of about 80 men to sail it. This photograph shows a replica of this famous ship. It shows three tall masts and their crow's-nests, the higher deck at the prow, known as the *fo'c'stle* (forecastle), and the tall layers of decks at the stern, known as the *aftercastle*. Originally named the *Pelican*, it was renamed the *Golden Hind* (*hind* meaning 'deer') just before negotiating the dreaded Strait of Magellan. This was a political decision, since the *Golden Hind* was an emblem of Sir Christopher Hatton, one of the principal bankers funding the voyage! This replica of the *Golden Hind* is based in Brixham Harbour, in Devon, where Drake worked and lived. Another replica is moored on the River Thames in South London.

Discussing the photograph

▶ Look at the photograph and ask the children if they know what kind of ship is shown.
▶ Discuss where it is kept and ask if anyone has been on it (or the other replica).
▶ Talk about the size of the ship, how small it seems, and how many crew members were needed to sail it.
▶ Discuss the implications of it being wooden, in terms of maintenance.

▶ Look at the height of the masts and think about the sailors who had to climb up in all weathers to work on the sails or go into the crow's-nest. Discuss what it must have been like.
▶ See if the children can name parts of the ship, such as the *masts, decks, prow, stern, rudder, forecastle, aftercastle, rigging*, and explain what they are.
▶ Explain how the English galleons were smaller than the Spanish ones because they wanted speed and agility and relied more on their guns.

Activities
▶ Help the children locate and label on the timeline (see photocopiable page 76) when the *Golden Hind* was built.
▶ Organise them into small groups to find out more about the history of the ship, mentioning that it was originally called the *Pelican*. If they are using the Internet, suggest they highlight key words and phrases in any pages they print off.
▶ Look at the picture of 'Sir Francis Drake' (provided on the CD). Make a class book about him and the *Golden Hind*, adding stories, first-hand accounts and illustrations. Use the accounts and stories on photocopiable pages 77–9 for further information.
▶ Provide materials for the children to make models of Tudor sailing ships.

An English fighting ship

This is a modern illustration of a Tudor warship based on research by the National Maritime Museum in London. They have used a variety of historical sources, since no contemporary plan has ever been discovered. What is interesting is the number of different decks ranged in layers above the galley and the hold. In the hold, barrels and casks containing food and wine were stored. The weight was useful in providing ballast, which assisted in the stability of the ship. The guns can be seen on the main deck at the top, on the forecastle and aftercastle, and also on the gun deck below the main deck. The guns, therefore, could be used to fire in any direction, giving all-round cover to the ship. Every part of the ship would be loaded with supplies and guns, so that there was very little room below decks for the crew.

Some of the sailors had to climb the rigging to furl and unfurl the sails as well as to carry out repairs and act as lookouts in the crow's-nests at the tops of the two main masts. These were particularly skilled jobs, and men were likely to be killed if they fell to the deck or went overboard. Sailing ships at this time took a considerable time to turn, so that if anyone went overboard, it was unlikely that they could be saved. Tending to the rigging and rope ladders was an important job, and sailors were skilled at many crafts. Apart from manning the guns, the most important job was that of the caulkers, those in charge of keeping the ship and barrels watertight.

Discussing the picture
▶ Ask the children what kind of picture this is, for example a modern illustration; a cross-section of a Tudor warship.
▶ Ask them to count the number of masts and work out how many sails the ship could carry.
▶ Talk about the rope ladders, rigging and sheets (ropes); consider the skill needed in knowing how to use all of these properly.
▶ Tell the class that the sailors had to know how to make and repair all the things on the ship in case of accidents at sea, where there would be no one else to help.
▶ Encourage the children to count how many decks there were. Point out the very tall deck at the front of the ship and explain that this was called the forecastle – since it was high up it was rather like a castle on the ship.
▶ Get the children to name as many parts of the ship as they can – the *hull*, the *rudder*, the *decks*, and so on.
▶ Looking very closely at the small details, the children can begin to work out some of the things that had to be done on board ship, such as manning the guns, checking the supplies, furling the sails, cooking and eating, and so on.

Activities
▶ Ask the children to label this illustration with the correct names for the different parts of the ship.
▶ Discuss the particular jobs that had to be done on board ship (see also 'Food on board a Tudor ship' and 'Life on board ship' provided on the CD) and ask the children to think of words

and phrases to describe how it might have felt, for instance to be up on the masts furling the sails in bad weather. Set them the task of writing a short imaginative piece of writing from the perspective of a sailor who has nearly fallen from the rigging in a storm at sea.

▶ Encourage the children to imagine the sounds, sights and smells during a battle when all the guns were firing and the ship was being fired upon by the enemy. Provide them with materials to draw or paint imaginative scenes and then to write descriptive pieces about the experience.

▶ Give the children small books in which to write a diary from the point of view of one of the sailors with a particular job, such as the cook or the officer in charge of the gunners. Alternatively, they could write up a short 'ship's log' as if by the captain, using information collected from other sources such as the Internet.

Food on board a Tudor ship

In this modern reconstruction, the illustrator shows the large cooking pot and simple open fire used for preparing the food for the ship's crew down in the galley. The food would have been stored in wooden barrels to keep it dry and safe from rats and mice, which were common on early sailing ships. The food typically eaten by sailors in Tudor times included salt, or 'bully', beef, which was hard and very salty. It had to be soaked and then stewed for a long time to make it edible. Ships' biscuits, or 'hard tack', was another staple diet, sometimes the only food available if all else was spoiled in bad weather. There would also be salt fish, cheese, for as long as it lasted, beans, bacon and dried peas. Most of the food was preserved for long journeys by being either heavily salted or dried. Sometimes food would be preserved by keeping it in vinegar, or pickling it. As you can imagine, eating salty pickled food made the men very thirsty and when water was in short supply, this would be a cause of great distress.

It was difficult to keep food fresh on board ship, and in the early days of long sea journeys, it was not recognised that fresh food was even necessary. Sometimes live animals, including pigs and goats, would be taken on board for their milk and then their meat as it was needed. It was only in the 18th and 19th centuries that people began to understand the link between serious diseases, such as scurvy, and the lack of fresh fruit and vegetables.

Discussing the picture
▶ Ask the children to comment on what they see in this illustration.
▶ Look at the cook and discuss what he is doing. Talk about where and how the food is cooked on board ship, noting the dangers in this method.
▶ Point out where and how the food and drink is stored. Wine and water would have been kept in barrels. (See if the children notice the rat near the barrels.)
▶ Encourage the children to think about what would happen to the barrels if the ship was in very dry, hot weather, for example the wood might get dry and shrink, making the barrels leak. Explain the importance of the cooper and caulker, who kept the barrels in good repair and kept them watertight.
▶ Notice the huge cooking pot and discuss why it was so large.
▶ Discuss the size of the crew and the work of the cook. Ask the children if they think that all the ship's crew could eat at once.
▶ Tell the children about the types of food eaten on board, especially the dried, salted and pickled food. Ask them if they would like to eat food like this. Discuss why we do not need to have so much food like this now because of refrigeration.
▶ Can the children tell you why fresh water would have been a very precious thing at sea? Ask why it could be in short supply when the ship is surrounded by it. Tell the children about the Samuel Taylor Coleridge's poem 'The Rime of the Ancient Mariner', which includes the words *Water, water everywhere, nor any drop to drink* and ask them to think about the meaning of these lines.
▶ Ask the children if they would have liked to have been Tudor sailors.

Activities
▶ Build up a collection of books, resources and Internet materials for the children to refer to when working on Tudor ships. Ask them to make use of these to find out more about life on board ship. Divide the class into small groups and ask each group to find out about a different aspect of life, such as the food, the work, the crew's living conditions, illnesses and diseases they caught, and so on.

▶ Set the children the task of finding out what the men liked to drink and why water was difficult to keep on board ship. Use simple science books to find out about how foods perish if not stored safely or preserved.

▶ Read a short extract from Robert Louis Stevenson's *Treasure Island* (Puffin Books) about the experiences of the cabin boy on board ship.

▶ Challenge the children to imagine what it would have been like to have been a cabin boy and to be taken away to sea. Encourage them to use their best descriptive language to write about the food they had to eat while away. This could be in the form of a prose story or diary entries.

A captain of a ship

There would often be a number of officers on Tudor ships. There would be the leader of the expedition, who was sometimes not even a sailor, but might be, like Columbus, a merchant or explorer in search of trade. There would be the ship's captain, an experienced sailor, yet who might still not have any knowledge or understanding of navigation. The other officers would be the master and the pilot, who was often also the mate and who would ensure the ship was heading on the right course. Petty officers included the boatswain, who was in charge of the ship's gear, such as the sails, cables, anchors and rigging, and the steward in charge of the provisions, food, water, wine and firewood.

Occasionally other people equated with officer rank would be on board, such as botanists, whose task would be to study the flora and fauna of the new lands, write reports on these and bring back specimens. The only person to have a separate cabin, however, was the captain. The captain and officers tended to live in much better conditions than the rest of the crew. The officers may have had bunks against the ship's side in the steerage or at the after end of the main deck. When possible, their table would be furnished with fresh food and they would eat and drink well, often off the best tableware and in comfortable conditions, as far as was possible in such a confined space.

A common sailor

Ordinary seamen would usually have no separate sleeping quarters of their own. They had to find their own space on the deck where they slept and ate, and there would be great competition for the most comfortable spots, such as the top of the hatch. The reason for this was that the hatch was in the middle of the deck and was often the only flat part of the deck available. The rest of the deck was built with a camber to allow water to run down the decks quickly and off the ship through holes in the sides.

The seamen would all be experienced sailors and would also have another craft skill, such as rope making, sail mending and making, carpentry, caulking, and coopering (see above). The food of the ordinary seamen was generally poor in comparison with that of the officers and often led to the men becoming ill with diseases such as scurvy, brought on by a lack of fresh food containing vitamin C.

Captain's living quarters

The only person to have his own cabin was the captain, while other officers would sometimes work and eat in it with him. This cabin was extremely small and it is hard for us to imagine how officers managed to work and eat in such cramped conditions. Despite the lack of space, however, every effort was made that the cabin should have all modern conveniences: a small bed or 'cot', a table and chairs, a desk large enough for charts and maps to be spread out upon, and room of course for the captain's sea chest, where his own personal belongings would be stored. Apart from his wardrobe, the captain would have his weapons, navigational instruments, writing implements, lanterns, the ship's log, Bible and the charts and maps that were needed.

Discussing the pictures
▶ Compare the pictures of the captain and the common sailor, and ask the children to point out the key differences between them.
▶ Look at the way each is dressed and discuss how the common sailor's clothes seem far more practical and more suited to working on board ship.

▶ Consider the different equipment carried by the captain, for example he is armed with a sword; he carries a map; he has an astrolabe (an early navigational instrument).
▶ Compare this with the things provided for the common seaman.
▶ Think about how the officers might have kept all their expensive clothes smart; ask the children if they think they did.
▶ Look at the captain's cabin. Explain how very small it is, in fact almost the size of a cupboard!
▶ Find volunteers to point out all the furniture and equipment the men have managed to squeeze into the cabin.
▶ Ask the children to imagine what it was like when the officers came in to talk about the voyage with the captain.
▶ Talk about how the common sailors lived in comparison to the officers.

Activities

▶ Set up an interview situation in which children are in role as common sailors. Ask them to interview each other, asking them to give reasons for going to sea when it is so dangerous (it was not unusual for half of a ship's crew to die during a long voyage).
▶ Divide the class into two groups, one of which will write a description of the things taken to sea by officers and the captain, and the other which will write about the things taken by an ordinary seaman. At the end of the session, compare the descriptions they have produced.
▶ Ask the children to write an entry in the ship's log about a day in the voyage of Drake around the world. They will need to write from the point of view of Drake himself. Read the first-hand account by Francis Pretty of Drake's arrival in the Strait of Magellan (see photocopiable page 77) to provide a starting point for their text.

Life on board ship

While the captain and officers were busy with their planning of the route, the crew would be engaged with carrying out their orders. They would have to keep the decks clean and maintain the condition of the wooden hull, keeping it free of barnacles, since these impeded the ship's manoeuvrability in the water. They would have to respond quickly to instructions about furling and unfurling the sails, keep a lookout in the crow's-nests and keep the watch at night. Ropes and sails had to be kept in good repair and food had to be prepared. The ship's stores had to be constantly checked to ensure their condition was kept up and that there were enough supplies to get the crew to their next port of call. At times when they were becalmed, they would have kept themselves occupied with stories, perhaps about sea monsters, and with songs and games. It was almost impossible, however, for the men to keep clean in such cramped conditions and they would often be covered with lice and fleas. There were no lavatories, and most of the waste went into sand and rubble kept as ballast in the bilges, at the bottom of the ship, no doubt becoming quite unpleasant by the end of a long voyage.

Discussing the picture

▶ Discuss the perspective of a Tudor ship that is shown in this picture.
▶ Ask for volunteers to point out all the different tasks they can see the sailors involved with. Ask them where the officers and captain are.
▶ Ask others to think about the jobs that had to be done that cannot be seen in this picture, such as checking the ship was watertight, checking and counting the supplies, cleaning the guns, repairing damaged woodwork, cooking, making new ropes, catching fish, baling out water, and so on.
▶ Encourage the children to think about the kinds of entertainment the men may have made for themselves, for example singing, telling stories, playing dice, cards and other games, gambling, fishing, dancing, and so on.
▶ Tell the children about the discipline on board ship, and how it was very harsh. For example, sailors who stole would lose a hand; those who killed someone would be thrown overboard tied to the dead body.
▶ Discuss why ordinary people decided to go to sea.

Activities

▶ Provide a wide range of resources for the children to continue their research into life at sea and encourage them to write short accounts and draw illustrations of their findings. Suggest they look into areas that they know less about, such as punishments or food.

▶ Using this illustration together with 'An English fighting ship' (provided on the CD), make a large-scale cross-section of a Tudor warship for the classroom wall and display the children's writing and illustrations around it to show what happened on board ship.

▶ Set the children the task of working in pairs to write an entry in the daily journal of an ordinary seaman or perhaps the ship's boy, describing his working and leisure time.

Attacking a Spanish treasure ship

During the Elizabethan period there were many privateers, and indeed this was the early occupation of Francis Drake and his relative, John Hawkins. Privateering involved attacking foreign ships at sea. Sometimes just the cargo would be stolen, but often the privateers would steal both the ship and its contents. The English ships were smaller and more manoeuvrable than the large, heavy Spanish treasure ships, or carracks, which were built to hold as much cargo as possible. In addition, the small English ships carried large numbers of guns and were able to disable the Spanish ships in order to board them more easily. The ships would be pulled alongside with grappling irons and ropes, and the privateers and their crew would then leap from ship to ship, usually using the tall forecastle and aftercastle for this purpose, and engage in hand to hand fighting.

This illustration from the 19th century shows privateers preparing to board a Spanish ship from a small rowing boat, possibly in some kind of surprise attack away from the main fighting. It shows the armour and weapons of the privateers as well as the costume worn in Tudor times. Swords and daggers were used as well as early pistols and muskets.

The adventure of Thomas Moon

This 19th century engraving illustrates the attack on a Spanish ship in Chile, where Francis Drake and some of his men succeeded in overcoming the Spanish and stealing a large sum of money. Thomas Moon is among the attackers, and is reputed to have shouted at the Spanish seamen in their own language, alarming them all. Here we see Moon ordering them to lie down, while the rest of the English board the ship. The illustration is based on the famous account of Drake's adventures during his circumnavigation of the world, written by Francis Pretty, one of his Gentlemen at Arms (see the extract from Pretty on photocopiable page 78).

Discussing the pictures

▶ Look at both illustrations and discuss what is happening.

▶ Remind the children about Drake's adventures as a privateer or pirate, and explain that there were constant attacks against Spanish ships by English privateers.

▶ Discuss why this was, for example England and Spain were enemies; they were sometimes at war with each other; there were great riches to be gained by attacking the Spanish ships.

▶ Discuss why the Spanish ships were carrying treasure. Talk about the Spanish colonies in Central and South America, and how a great deal of silver and gold had been found there, which the Spanish were bringing back to Spain in ships.

▶ Talk about the Spanish treasure fleets, whose groups of large, slow-moving ships were easy to catch and board.

▶ Ask whether it was right for privateers to do these things; consider whether people in Tudor times held the same views about these things as we do now.

Activities

▶ Read the account of Francis Pretty about the Thomas Moon incident (see photocopiable page 78), using the pictures to illustrate the story. Discuss the amount of treasure which Drake and his men seized during these exploits. Make a word bank of all the words to describe how the men felt when they realised how much they had gained and that Drake was to give them all a share.

▶ Set the children the task of writing a letter from the Spanish monarch to Queen Elizabeth, complaining about the treatment of Spanish ships at the hands of the English privateers. Ask them to start and end the letter with very elaborate, highly respectful phrases.

▶ Provide materials for the children to create their own posters advertising an exciting life in the Queen's navy, using some of the above information and illustrations.

▶ Take the hot seat as Queen Elizabeth or one of her naval commanders, and answer the children's questions about the activities of some of the English captains like Drake and Hawkins.

Treasure chest

This is an example of an old sea chest. They were used to hold the captain's personal belongings securely and were usually locked with a large heavy padlock. The chests would have been made of strong oak, lined with leather all bound together and sealed with bands of metal. This chest appears to have been fastened in two places and has elaborately designed handles. The inside of the lid is made up of intricately woven pieces of leather, possibly to create small storage spaces for precious or secret items. These chests could also be used, of course, for storing treasure taken from Spanish ships.

Treasure

This is a photograph of the kind of treasure that might have been taken from a Spanish galleon by Tudor privateers. Gold coins like these, sometimes referred to as *dubloons*, were highly prized and each one very valuable in Tudor times. Very often, however, gold and silver would have been transported by the Spanish in the form of bars. All kinds of items made of gold would have been melted down into solid bars, since this made storage much easier. In this way, many precious artefacts, both religious and everyday, that belonged to the South American Indian peoples were lost for ever.

Discussing the pictures

▶ Look first at the picture of the chest, and ask if anyone has seen one of these before. Explain that this was known as a sea chest, or sometimes a treasure chest.
▶ Ask the children if they can think what it would have been used for if it were a sea chest.
▶ Talk about what a sea captain like Francis Drake would have done if he had gained a lot of treasure on a raid, for example he might have emptied his sea chest to put in the treasure; maybe he took empty chests on his voyages to put the treasure into.
▶ Look at the photograph of the hoard of coins, and explain to the children that there really was a lot of treasure to be had in Tudor times.
▶ Tell them about the Spanish colonies in South America and remind them about the Spanish treasure fleets.
▶ Explain that the coins might have been *pesos* if they were from Mexico, or they might have been called *ducats* if they were Spanish coins. The English used *dubloons*.
▶ Tell the children that very often, the treasure would be in other forms, such as gold bars, precious stones, wine or other exotic products from faraway places.
▶ Ask the children to imagine what sailors must have felt when they found treasure chests.

Activities

▶ Read extracts from *Treasure Island* by Robert Louis Stevenson (Puffin Books), especially parts where 'pieces of eight' are discussed.
▶ Ask the children if they can think of any other stories about treasure. They could read Philip Pullman's retelling of the story of Aladdin, *Aladdin and the Enchanted Lamp* (Scholastic: Hippo).
▶ Suggest that they write their own adventures about treasure hunting.
▶ Organise the children into pairs to make treasure maps or charts. Set them the task of producing a key and creating symbols to illustrate their maps.

Gold funerary mask

Made in pre-Columbian South America, this gold face mask was brought to Europe during early voyages of the Spanish explorers. Explorers like Columbus were keen to take back these kinds of objects to show their sponsors back home in Spain the sort of treasure that they could have if they funded other expeditions. The mask gives us an idea of what the ancient peoples of this part of the world looked like. This face has filled teeth and a nose ornament, sometimes called a nose plug, and closed eyes, suggesting inward reflection. Many peoples of South America wore nose plugs of gold and these were highly coveted by the European explorers in search of treasure. Nose and ear piercing was traditional among the Amerindians in Central and South America, and the jewellery they wore was usually of gold. The ancient people of the region knew of many ways of working with metal. This mask appears to have been made using the 'lost wax' method, which could mould very detailed objects such as this.

Discussing the mask

▶ Look at the mask and ask the children where they think it may have come from.
▶ Discuss its characteristics, and if necessary explain that it came from a country called Colombia in South America.
▶ Ask what they think it is made from, and why it was taken away. Explain that it was more likely to have been stolen than given as a gift.
▶ Discuss how historians know that it is from Colombia, for example the facial features which are those of the Native South Americans; the way that the mask was made.
▶ Explain that items like these date back to before the time of Columbus, so they are very old. They could date back to between 600 and 1100AD, which is the equivalent of the early Middle Ages in Europe.
▶ Ask the children to look again very closely at the detail of the mask, in particular the teeth and jewellery.

Activities

▶ Help the class to locate and label the dates on the timeline (see photocopiable page 76) when this mask may have been made and when it was taken to Europe by the explorers. Tell them that it can now be seen in the British Museum in London.
▶ Make papier mâché masks and spray them or paint them with gold paint. Use these to decorate a class display about explorers.
▶ Tell the class that this is known as a *funerary* mask. Ask them to look up the meaning and use of a funerary mask.

Native Americans in Virginia

In 1584 Sir Walter Raleigh received glowing accounts of the Americas and was determined to send a colonising expedition. The expedition set off in 1585 and landed in America in August 1585. The area was named Virginia in honour of Queen Elizabeth and a colony was set up on Roanoke Island. The initial colonisers consisted only of men and were therefore later joined by a number of families and a few children. However, by 1591 the colony had vanished and no trace of the settlers was found. It is not known what happened to the 'lost colony'. The settlers had initially had friendly relations with the Native Americans but these had deteriorated. The war with the Spanish had also meant that promised supplies from England had not materialised. Some evidence indicated that the settlers had possibly moved elsewhere but this was never proved.

This 16th century painting gives a particular impression of what the indigenous people of North America were like when the first settlers arrived. The artist has portrayed them as fairly primitive people in their dress, appearance and behaviour. Their costume is very basic, essentially consisting of a simple loincloth for both men and women. They wear no ornamentation or headdresses at all other than a feather in the man's hair. They are cooking out in the open on the ground around a huge pot – while the man fans the flames of the fire, the woman tends to the cooking. The picture indicates that the artist probably viewed the peoples of the Americas as savages, conforming to the ideas about other world civilisations prevalent during that period in Europe.

Native Americans in a cave dwelling

In sharp contrast to the previous picture, the indigenous peoples of Virginia in this picture are shown housed in relatively spacious accommodation, comfortably furnished with woven rugs and mats. The women are seated on chairs and are well dressed in long skirts, shawls, leggings and shoes. They are wearing jewellery in the form of bracelets, necklaces and ornate headdresses. Their clothes have skilful designs and patterns and have fringed edges. The men wear similarly ornate clothing, with elaborate feather headdresses, denoting their status as either chief or warrior. The people are well equipped with tools, purses, a smoking pipe and weapons of several kinds. Above all, the Native Americans are portrayed as cultured, compassionate people, caring for the stricken white man, whom they have made comfortable and are trying to care for.

Like the picture described above, this 19th century picture may also be influenced by the more romantic views held at the time in which it was created. But it provides an excellent image to compare with the 16th century painting.

Discussing the pictures

▶ Show the two pictures to the children and ask them to decide which they think was made earlier, and is older, and which is the later picture. Ask them to explain why, for example the earlier one has Latin writing on it; the style of artwork looks more old-fashioned.

▶ Discuss what the pictures intend to show, for example everyday life of the Native Americans in the state of Virginia.

▶ Explain that the settlement of Sir Walter Raleigh, Roanoke, was set up in Virginia.

▶ Ask the children to point out the major differences between the two illustrations – in costume, context, dwelling, equipment, behaviour, and so on.

▶ Discuss the impression that is given of the indigenous people by the early picture, and think about why this was.

▶ Discuss the impression given by the second picture, and again discuss why this was.

Activities

▶ Talk about the notion of interpretation and discuss the idea that interpretations can change over time. Sometimes the interpretations of what things were like reflect more about the people who made the pictures than about the subject of the pictures. Get the class to think of all the different kinds of interpretations they have seen or heard of the Native North Americans and make a list of these.

▶ If possible, find examples of different interpretations, such as in comics, feature films from the past and present day, or from old school books. Ask the children to note how the interpretations differ.

▶ Challenge the children to work in pairs to produce an argument for or against the accuracy of one or other of the two pictures on the CD.

NOTES ON THE PHOTOCOPIABLE PAGES

Word and sentence cards
PAGES 73–5

A number of specific types of vocabulary have been introduced on the word and sentence cards, including words associated with:

▶ exploration, such as *discovery, voyage, circumnavigate, circumnavigation*

▶ colonisation, such as *trade, colony, indigenous, empire*

▶ life at sea, such as *bow, stern, captain, crew, knot*.

The children should be encouraged to think of other appropriate words to add to those provided, in order to build up a word bank for the theme of the Tudor explorers. They could include words encountered in their researches, such as *privateer, sailors, booty*, in relation to the personal history of some of the explorers. They could also use the cards in labelling displays and in writing simple and complex sentences to record what they have learned. They should also use the word cards as support in descriptive, factual and creative work and in writing discussions.

Activities

▶ Once you have made copies of the word and sentence cards, cut them out and laminate them, using them as often as possible when talking about the Tudor explorers. They could be used for word games and spelling games, or to assist less able readers in making up their own sentences or phrases.

▶ Add further vocabulary to the set of words, using those suggested by the children.

▶ Make displays of aspects of Tudor exploration and use word and sentence cards to label and describe them.

▶ Encourage the children to read the labels and sentences to yourself, adult helpers and visitors to the classroom.

▶ Encourage the children to use the words in stories and non-fiction writing as often as possible.

▶ Organise times during whole-class plenaries to practise reading the sentence cards together. Follow up this activity with pairs of children reading the sentences. Check which words each child can read. Ask the children to create new sentences of their own.

► Add the words to a class word bank, and encourage the children to copy or write them frequently, for example when doing their own extended writing.

► Make wordsearches and crossword puzzles for the children to complete using specific sets of words related to the current topic, such as words to do with the voyages.

► Make cloze procedure sheets, omitting the key words from the text. Encourage the children to write and spell the words without support.

► Devise '20 questions' and 'Hangman' games based on the key words.

Tudor exploration timeline
PAGE 76

This timeline can be used to introduce children to the notion of chronology over a specific, recognisable span of time, in this case the period of Tudor exploration. The information it contains can be adapted according to the age and interests of the children and it could be used as the basis of a large wall timeline, to which children could add more detail as they work on the topic.

This timeline could be used alongside maps, portraits and illustrations about the Tudor explorers to give children some visual representation of chronological sequence. It could be adapted in the form of a long string which could be stretched across the classroom, to represent the distance in time covered by the period. Alternatively, it could be adapted to create a large wall frieze to which pictures of different characters and events could be added as the children learn about them.

The kind of timeline shown here can also be useful at the end of a topic, for checking children's success in grasping ideas of sequence, chronology and understanding of the use of dates. This particular timeline will be useful also in discussions about the reasons why all the information is so close together. Children could also be asked to create their own version of a Tudor explorers' timeline.

Discussing the timeline
► At the beginning of the topic, ask the children what they think this timeline shows.
► Clarify what the dates on the timeline mean.
► Explain that this line with dates and pictures represents the passing of time.
► Talk about the key events during the Tudor period of exploration, and add more labels and events as appropriate.
► Use the stories and accounts of life and events at sea, and the pictures provided on the CD to illustrate the discussion about the timeline.

Activities
► Make a class timeline, using the timeline on photocopiable page 76 as an example. Ask the children to put on any other pictures or portraits from the period they find, in the appropriate places on the timeline. Build up a more detailed illustrated timeline as the topic progresses.
► Tell stories from the history of the Tudor explorers and use the pictures from the CD when looking at the timeline.
► Give the children a blank timeline, or a section of the timeline, with either relevant dates or words and ask them to draw or paste onto it relevant pictures in the right places.

The Strait of Magellan
PAGE 77

This extract from an account written by one of Francis Drake's men at the time of Drake's circumnavigation of the world describes the harsh conditions and some of the sights they saw in the stormy Strait of Magellan at the southern tip of South America. The children will need to find where this place is and to consider what the weather is like there. Some of the language in the account will seem very strange to the children and it may need some explanation (see Discussing the text below).

Discussing the text
► Look at the title of the extract, and ask the children if they have heard of this place before. Explain briefly where it is.
► Read through the text with the children, who will probably need to listen to it and read it more than once.
► Ask for volunteers to summarise each paragraph in their own words.

▶ Ask what words the children found difficult or strange. Pick out those which they may be able to work out for themselves from the context, such as *shuttings-up, whereof, whereunto* and *carrieth*.

▶ Ask the children to point out words and expressions they are unable to work out and give them simple explanations of their meanings, for example *clean consumed* – eaten away; *lack their best commodity* – their best feature is missing; *league* – about three miles; *victualled ourselves thoroughly* – ate well.

▶ Look at the phrases which are almost the same as in modern English, but just worded in a slightly different way, such as *there be many fair harbours; this Strait is extreme cold; we found great store of fowl*. See if any volunteers can say these phrases in modern English without changing their meaning.

▶ Talk about the excitement these sailors must have experienced at seeing strange lands for the first time.

▶ Ask the children to pick out the parts of the text which reflect the surprise or interest of the writer.

▶ Consider what it must have been like for sailors living out on deck with no heating, or very little, in such conditions – the cold winds, frostbite and so on. (See also the image of the Golden Hind provided on the CD.)

Activities

▶ Challenge the children to find the Strait of Magellan on a globe of the world or 'Modern world map' (provided on the CD). Ask them to describe its location in their own words.

▶ Help them to locate the dates of Drake's voyage around the world and label it on the class timeline.

▶ Provide art materials or collage materials for them to create their ideas of what the huge ice mountains looked like.

▶ Set up a role play in which half the class, in the role of interviewers, can ask questions of the others, who take on the role of the explorers, returned home.

The adventure of Thomas Moon and others   PAGE 78

This first-hand account tells the adventures of some of the English men who encountered the Spanish in Chile. Seeking out one of their ships, they first boarded it and then, after taking what they wanted from the town of Santiago, stole it. This was the expected behaviour of adventurers in those days. They would join an expedition partly in order to gain what they could in the way of booty, or goods that they could steal in the course of their adventures. This activity was called privateering. Privateering was a method for trading ships in time of war whereby a privately owned, manned and armed ship could operate on the high seas as a conventional warship. In the event of capturing ships they were entitled to a substantial share of its cargo. The remainder went to the Crown. As in the previous text, there are archaic words and phrases in this text which may need explanation.

Discussing the text

▶ Discuss the title of this text and explain to the children who Thomas Moon was, then read it through to and with the children.

▶ Discuss what happens in the first paragraph and then ask for volunteers to explain what the men do in each of the other paragraphs.

▶ Talk about the meaning of the words *adventurer, explorer* and *privateer* (see above).

▶ Discuss the expectations of men who joined adventures such as Drake's.

▶ Tell the children a little about Drake's past, and how he first worked as a privateer.

▶ Discuss what his men did in this adventure, and whether the children think they were right or not.

▶ Explain how England and Spain were enemies at the time, and how this may have made the men feel justified in what they were doing.

▶ Talk about what Spanish sailors might have done if the situation had been reversed.

▶ Ask the children how Drake and the men probably felt about what they had done.

▶ Discuss why they would have wanted to take the sheep that they found, as well as the silver.

▶ Consider the way they treated the people that they came across, for example *We took the silver and left the man*.

Activities

▶ Review the date of this adventure, during Drake's circumnavigation of the world, and help the children to locate Chile and Santiago on 'Modern world map' (provided on the CD).

▶ Challenge the children to research more detail about Drake's life and the voyage around the world. Ask them to create a timeline of their own, working in pairs, either about Drake's life, or about the circumnavigation of the globe.

▶ Use the illustration of 'The adventure of Thomas Moon' (provided on the CD) in conjunction with the account, and set the children the task of writing the adventure in their own words. Write out the phrase *Abaxo perro!* (meaning 'Go down, dog') for them on the board. Explain that *Abaxo* may be an old-fashioned way of spelling the word *abajo*, or perhaps a guess or mistake made by the writer.

Attitudes to circumnavigation PAGE 79

This account explains how beliefs about the world changed, and how often educated people, even in ancient times, had a clear idea about the shape of the world. It also explains the mistake that Columbus made, in thinking that he had arrived in the East, when in fact he had arrived on the shore of America. He had made this mistake because he thought the world was smaller in circumference than it actually was. The account shows how man's ability to circumnavigate the globe has changed dramatically in the more recent past.

Discussing the text

▶ Read through the text with the class.

▶ Ask the children to try to recall the people who have circumnavigated the world. Discuss how long this took Drake (approximately three years) and compare this with modern times, when a space shuttle can orbit the Earth in 90 minutes.

▶ Discuss the meaning of the word *circumnavigate*.

▶ Talk about the knowledge of people in ancient times.

▶ Look at the map of Ptolemy on the CD and consider the opinion that educated people knew quite a lot about the world's geography a very long time ago.

▶ Discuss how much of this knowledge was lost and how people living in Europe much later on, for example in the Middle Ages, had less knowledge than some of the Ancient Greeks, and different beliefs about the order of the world.

▶ Explain how educated people like Columbus knew that the world was a sphere, while some people at that time may not have believed this.

▶ Ask the children if they can explain what Columbus' mistake was; where did he think he had arrived in 1492?

▶ Explain that this was why he called the Caribbean islands the *Indies*.

▶ Discuss how the error may partly have been to do with his miscalculation of the Earth's circumference. He thought he had gone all round when he had only gone part of the way round, because he thought the Earth was smaller than it actually is.

Activities

▶ Help the children to place the events mentioned in the account on a class timeline.

▶ Ask the children to list ways in which man's ability to travel around the globe has improved.

▶ Give the children a homework task of finding out about people who have travelled around the world in recent times, and ask them to bring to school some of their names.

▶ Challenge the children to carry out their own research in groups and find out more about one or two of the following: Ptolemy, Magellan, Columbus, Amerigo Vespucci, and the people who have circumnavigated the world in recent times. Ask them to make notes on their findings in preparation for a brief talk to the class.

The settlement of Sir Walter Raleigh PAGE 80

This account tells of the attempts of Sir Walter Raleigh to set up a settlement in North America. There was considerable interest at the time and people were prepared to set out on an adventure and a new life. However, what made it difficult to establish a settlement at first seems to have been the slowness of transport. Combined with the warfare going on at the time and continuing difficult relationships with the Spanish, the lack of reinforcements and supplies made it difficult for settlers to survive for very long.

Discussing the text

▶ Read through the text with the children.

▶ Ask them what kind of family Raleigh came from, and how this was different from Francis Drake, who came from a farming family.

▶ Ask them in what part of the world Raleigh wished to set up his new settlement.

▶ Ask for volunteers to suggest reasons why early settlers struggled to survive, for example lack of food they were used to; conflicts with the native population; lack of other supplies such as tools for making things.

▶ Discuss what other problems they might have faced in a new land, such as not knowing what to grow and eat; not being able to communicate with the people who lived there; being afraid of the native peoples.

▶ Discuss what often happened to adventurers when they arrived in new places, for example attacks by the Spanish or by local people; they caught diseases.

▶ Ask the children why Raleigh was eventually executed.

▶ Discuss the meaning of words such as *treason, disputes, noble, court* and *favourite*.

▶ Tell the children that today there is still a town called City of Raleigh on Roanoke Island.

Activities

▶ Help the children to locate the State of Virginia and Roanoke on a map of North America. Help them to find the date of Raleigh's attempted settlement and to label this on a class timeline.

▶ As part of a whole-class lesson in ICT, use the Internet to look up the *City of Raleigh* and *Roanoke* on the Internet. Display the web page on a large screen or whiteboard so that the whole class can see it. Encourage the children to make their own notes from what is displayed.

▶ Take the hot seat as Sir Walter Raleigh and encourage the children to devise and ask you questions about your childhood, youth and later life. Make sure that they include questions about the decision to execute you.

▶ Discuss and compare the treatment of Sir Francis Drake and Sir Walter Raleigh after their various dealings with the Spanish. Ask the children to write a brief comparison of what they did and how this was responded to in England. To challenge the more able, ask them to give reasons for this very different treatment at home of the two men, including the attitudes of the monarchs.

Exploration word cards

exploration

discovery

voyage

circumnavigate

circumnavigation

Drake was the first captain to return with his crew after circumnavigating the world.

Colonisation word cards

trade

colony

indigenous

empire

Amerindian

Amerindians are the native or indigenous
peoples of America.

Life at sea word cards

bow	**stern**
captain	**crew**
knot	**lead and line**
scurvy	**boatswain**
clinker	**forecastle**

Some nautical terms such as 'travelling at 20 *knots*' have their origins in very simple methods used on Tudor sailing ships.

READY RESOURCES ▶▶ H I S T O R Y

Tudor exploration timeline

EXPLORERS FROM PORTUGAL AND SPAIN

EXPLORERS FROM BRITAIN

1400

1488
Bartholemew Diaz rounds the Cape of Good Hope

1492
Columbus sails to the Caribbean

1495
Vasco da Gama sails to the Caribbean

1497
The Cabots reach Newfoundland

1500

1513
Balboa sights the Pacific

1521
Magellan sets sail around the world

1553
Chancellor makes trade links with Russia

1576
Frobisher reaches Hudson Bay

1577–1580
Drake circumnavigates the world

1584
Raleigh begins to set up Roanoke colony

1600

Illustration © Nova Developments

The Strait of Magellan

The 17th day of August we departed the port of St. Julian, and the 20th day we fell with the Strait of Magellan, going into the South Sea; at the cape or headland whereof we found the body of a dead man, whose flesh was clean consumed. The 21st day we entered the Strait, which we found to have many turnings, and as it were shuttings-up, as if there were no passage at all. By means whereof we had the wind often against us; so that some of the fleet recovering a cape or point of land, others should be forced to turn back again, and to come to an anchor where they could.

In this Strait there be many fair harbours, with store of fresh water. But yet they lack their best commodity, for the water there is of such depth, that no man shall find ground to anchor in, except it be in some narrow river or corner, or between some rocks; so that if any extreme blasts or contrary winds do come, whereunto the place is much subject, it carrieth with it no small danger. The land on both sides is very huge and mountainous; the lower mountains whereof, although they be monstrous and wonderful to look upon for their height, yet there are others which in height exceed them in a strange manner, reaching themselves above their fellows so high, that between them did appear three regions of clouds. These mountains are covered with snow.

This Strait is extreme cold, with frost and snow continually; the trees seem to stoop with the burden of the weather, and yet are green continually, and many good and sweet herbs do very plentifully grow and increase under them. The breadth of the Strait is in some places a league, in some other places two leagues and three leagues, and in some other four leagues; but the narrowest place hath a league over.

The 24th of August we arrived at an island in the Straits, where we found great store of fowl which could not fly, of the bigness of geese; whereof we killed in less than one day 3,000, and victualled ourselves thoroughly therewith.

from *Sir Francis Drake's Famous Voyage Around the World, 1580* by Francis Pretty, one of Drake's Gentlemen at Arms

The adventure of Thomas Moon and others

When we came thither we found, indeed, the ship (that they had been told about) riding at anchor, having in her eight Spaniards and three negroes; who, thinking us to have been Spaniards, and their friends, welcomed us with a drum, and made ready a botija (jar) of wine of Chili to drink to us. But as soon as we were entered, one of our company called Thomas Moon began to lay about him, and struck one of the Spaniards, and said unto him, "Abaxo, perro!" that is, in English "Go down, dog!" One of these Spaniards, seeing persons of that quality in those seas, all to crossed and blessed himself. But, to be short, we stowed them under hatches, all save one Spaniard, who suddenly and desperately leapt overboard into the sea, and swam ashore to the town of Santiago, to give them warning of our arrival.

They of the town, being not above nine households, presently fled away and abandoned the town. Our General manned his boat and the Spanish ship's boat, and went to the town; and, being come to it, we rifled it, and came to a small chapel, which we entered, and found therein a silver chalice, two cruets, and one altar-cloth, the spoil whereof our General gave to Master Fletcher, his minister. We found also in this town a warehouse stored with wine of Chili and many boards of cedar-wood; all which wine we brought away with us, and certain of the boards to burn for firewood. And so, being come aboard, we departed the haven, having first set all the Spaniards on land, saving one John Griego, a Greek born, whom our General carried with him as pilot to bring him into the haven of Lima.

When we were at sea our General rifled the ship, and found in her good store of the wine of Chili, and 25,000 pesos of very pure and fine gold of Valdivia, amounting in value to 37,000 ducats of Spanish money, and above.

From hence we went to a certain port called Tarapaca; where, being landed, we found by the sea side a Spaniard lying asleep, who had lying by him thirteen bars of silver, which weighed 4,000 ducats Spanish. We took the silver and left the man.

Not far from hence, going on land for fresh water, we met with a Spaniard and an Indian boy driving eight llamas or sheep of Peru, which are as big as asses; every of which sheep had on his back two bags of leather, each bag containing 50 lb. weight of fine silver. So that, bringing both the sheep and their burthen to the ships, we found in all the bags eight hundred weight of silver.

from *Sir Francis Drake's Famous Voyage Around the World, 1580* by Francis Pretty, one of Drake's Gentlemen at Arms

Attitudes to circumnavigation

For many years before Christopher Columbus set sail, some people believed that the Earth was like a disc, with Jerusalem at its centre. This idea of the world is shown on the different versions of the Mappa Mundi that still exist today. These people did fear that, although not exactly flat, there was an end to the world and that it would be dangerous to sail too near to it. Others, particularly the scholars from ancient times, already knew that the Earth was shaped like a sphere. The map of Ptolemy shows us this. They had realised that the horizon was not a straight line and that ships sailing into the distance disappeared over the horizon, yet they were safe and returned eventually.

Although scholars knew that the Earth was round, they did not know a great deal about the land areas on its surface nor how large these areas of land were. They did not know the size of the oceans nor how far it was around the whole of the Earth's circumference.

Columbus was one of a few educated people who understood that if you travelled around a globe, then you must return eventually to your starting point. He knew, therefore, that to get to the east you could sail east, but you could also sail west. Columbus spent much time studying maps and charts and learning about navigation – how to find your way across an ocean where there are no landmarks to show where you are. Columbus was sure he could navigate around the globe, from west to east.

Many people were not convinced. Columbus had wanted to prove this theory for many years, and had asked all kinds of people to support him with funds for a voyage. He had asked King Henry of Portugal, whom he knew to be interested in exploration, but he had turned him down. He had also asked King Henry VII of England, but had been turned down again. On several occasions he had asked Queen Isabella and King Ferdinand of Spain for help, but they had also refused. Columbus seemed to be alone in his desire to prove that sailing west was a safe route to the east.

Finally, however, Spain's long war against the Moors came to an end, and Ferdinand and Isabella were prepared to listen to Columbus's idea. They agreed to fund his adventure, and he was at last able to try to prove himself correct.

However, in 1492 Columbus came across a comletely unknown land. He tried to convince himself and others that he had arrived in the east, and called the islands he found the Indies, and the people Indians, but eventually he had to accept that this was a new land to the west of Europe. It was a bitter moment for Columbus, no doubt, when Amerigo Vespucci was credited with the discovery of the new continent and it was named America after him.

The first circumnavigation was not completed until one of Ferdinand Magellan's ships, which set out in 1519, returned home. Sir Francis Drake was the first to bring back his crew after sailing around the world between 1577 and 1580. In modern times it is much easier for people to race around the world and to sail around it single-handed. The idea of going quickly around the world has inspired stories such as *Around the World in Eighty Days* by Jules Verne, and also prompted people to try to go around the world in a balloon. Spaceships, of course, can orbit the Earth in much shorter time!

Illustration © Nova Developments

The settlement of Sir Walter Raleigh

In 1584, Sir Walter Raleigh paid for a voyage of exploration to North America, where he had been granted the right to explore. He sent two experienced captains, Armadas and Barlowe, who soon found land. Raleigh named the land that they found Virginia. They returned to Court saying the land was good and the natives were friendly. They brought home two native Americans and plants, including potato and tobacco plants, which were a huge success in England. Raleigh was knighted in 1585 and a new colony in Virginia was planned. This was the famous colony of Roanoke.

Early settlers had struggled to live successfully on Roanoke Island, but Raleigh arrived with another group to establish a settlement. It was their task to found the 'City of Raleigh'. The settlers took over the deserted fort, left by their countrymen, built timber cabins, cleared land and planted it. However, more supplies were needed from England if the community was to survive the whole year round.

John White, elected leader of the community, decided to sail to England himself to get the necessary supplies. But when he reached home, he found that England was engaged in a bitter war with Spain and all efforts were being put into dealing with the strength of the Spanish Armada. Nobody was interested in the plight of a handful of settlers in far distant America. It was two years before he could lead a relief expedition. On his return, he found no trace of the settlers he had left there.

In 1595, Raleigh set out on another expedition to South America, looking for a legendary ancient city known as El Dorado, which people thought was rich in gold. On this voyage, he discovered Guyana and returned home to write an account of the journey.

After some problems with the new monarch, King James, Raleigh was allowed to return to South America to search for El Dorado, provided he did not upset the Spanish in the area. This was important, as James was anxious to end the long series of conflicts with Spain. When the ships arrived, Raleigh was too ill to go ashore. His son, Walter, was one of those that went. Walter and his comrades unfortunately got into a fight with some Spaniards and Walter was killed. Hearing the news, Raleigh sadly sailed home. However, when he arrived he was put in prison for breaking his promise to the king and fighting the Spanish. He was executed for this treasonable behaviour in 1618.

Photograph © Nova Developments